P9-DXT-880

KNIT
Baby Blankets!

Edited by
GWEN STEEGE

Storey Publishing

The mission of Storey Publishing is to serve our customers by publishing practical information that encourages personal independence in harmony with the environment.

Edited by Gwen Steege, Masha Zager, and Karen Levy
Art direction, cover, and text design by Susi Oberhelman
Cover photograph by Ross Whitaker
Interior photographs by Zeva Oelbaum
Illustrations by Alison Kolesar
Text production by Jennifer Jepson Smith
Indexed by Eileen M. Clawson

Copyright © 2003 by Storey Publishing, LLC

All rights reserved. No part of this book may be reproduced without written permission from the publisher, except by a reviewer who may quote brief passages or reproduce illustrations in a review with appropriate credits; nor may any part of this book be reproduced, stored in a retrieval system, or transmitted in any form or by any means — electronic, mechanical, photocopying, recording, or other — without written permission from the publisher.

The information in this book is true and complete to the best of our knowledge. All recommendations are made without guarantee on the part of the editor or Storey Publishing. The editor and publisher disclaim any liability in connection with the use of this information. For additional information, please contact Storey Publishing, 210 MASS MoCA Way, North Adams, MA 01247.

Storey books are available for special premium and promotional uses and for customized editions. For further information, please call 1-800-793-9396.

Printed in Hong Kong by Elegance Printing

10 9 8 7 6 5 4 3 2 1

Library of Congress Cataloging-in-Publication Data

Knit baby blankets! / edited by Gwen Steege.
     p. cm.
Includes index.
ISBN 1-58017-495-7 (alk. paper)
1. Knitting—Patterns. 2. Blankets. 3. Infants' supplies. I. Steege, Gwen, 1940–

TT825.K6227 2003
746.43'20437-dc21

2003042509

Contents

All Covered Up

It's hard to think of any sight more likely to melt your heart than a sleeping infant tucked peacefully under a blanket in her crib or carriage. Babies break down all barriers and, like magnets, draw friendly remarks and admiring glances, even from perfect strangers.

This book contains a collection of baby blanket designs from North American knitters. It features both simple, quick-to-knit projects for first-time or on-the-go knitters as well as more complex multicolor or textured knits that give experienced knitters an opportunity to show off their skills and create a true heirloom that will be appreciated by generations of babies.

Handle with Care

If your baby blanket is a gift, include instructions for how to care for the blanket with the package. You might want to recommend that parents be particularly careful to remove all soap when laundering the blanket, as soap residue can irritate a baby's tender skin; excess soap may also mat the yarn fibers. Stains are often the curse of young parents' laundry experience. You can suggest that they try soaking the blanket in cold water while the stain is still wet before laundering as usual.

Baby blankets are ideal projects for experimenting with designs that may at first seem to be something of a challenge, since most are relatively small and, unlike garments, require no fitting or shaping. Some of the projects included here are made in sections, then pieced together; these make great take-along projects. Don't hesitate to try new yarns and techniques. No matter which design you choose, your blanket is sure to be loved and used for years to come.

You won't want to stop at making just one. Every baby needs a cuddly blanket that is like a warm hug that soothes him to sleep; it may also turn out to be that favorite and indispensable "blankie" that goes everywhere with him. Whether you are swaddling baby in a simple stretchy receiving blanket after a bath or tucking her snugly under a thick and warmly felted carriage robe for a winter outing, you'll cherish each hand-knit blanket. They are perfectly practical and wonderfully welcome gifts for babies everywhere. Babies are such an amazing gift — let's wrap them richly!

A Yarn by Any Name

If you haven't visited a yarn store recently, you're in for a delightful treat, with temptations on each shelf and in every bin — explosions of color, texture, and fiber all there for the choosing. It's important that yarns for baby knits be washable and comfortable, but other than those considerations, the sky's the limit. Think beyond the usual pastels to rich jewel tones, jazzy variegations, or bold contrasting colors. Red, black, and white are sometimes promoted as ideal colors for attracting baby's attention and encouraging some kinds of developmental progress. Explore the various novelty yarns for special effects, and ask about yarns developed especially for babies for their extra softness or washability.

Base your selection on the blanket's use and your own preferences. Will this blanket be used to swaddle a newborn and therefore need to be super soft? Or should it be thick and warm and fit into a carriage or stroller for a crisp fall outing? The blankets pictured in this book were knitted with cottons or washable wools, with some novelty yarns as accents. Some of the new man-made fibers are preferred by many knitters and parents because they are not only extremely soft, but also completely easy-care. Each project includes information about the yarns we used to create the blankets, but feel free to use other yarns that give you the correct knitting gauge.

Many knitters prefer natural fibers for their hand-knits. For instance, even when wet, wool is usually warmer than cotton or acrylic, but babies may find wool itchy or even be allergic to it. If wool is your preference, look for washable wools that are not only softer, but also processed so that they can be machine washed. Often labeled "superwash," these must be washed and dried at

Knitter's Talk

To make instructions more concise, most knitters use abbreviations. If you're new to knitting, they can seem like a foreign language. We have avoided overusing abbreviations in this book. Here's what you'll find:

cc	contrasting color
cm	centimeter
cn	cable needle
cont	continue
dec	decrease/decreasing
dp	double point
inc	increase/increasing
K	knit
K2tog	knit 2 stitches together
M1	make 1
mc	main color
mm	millimeter
P	purl
P2tog	purl 2 stitches together
psso	pass slip stitch over
sl	slip
ssk	slip, slip, knit the 2 slipped stitches together
st(s)	stitch(es)
St st	stockinette stitch (knit 1 row, purl 1 row)
yb	yarn back
yf	yarn forward
yd(s)	yard(s)

ALL COVERED UP

the temperature and setting stated on the yarn label. Note that if you're making a felted project, you can't use washable wool, as it won't shrink.

Cotton, or a cotton blend, is a favorite of many knitters who prefer natural fibers. A cotton blanket is ideal for a spring or summer baby, as it's not only washable but also lighter weight than a comparable wool. Look for soft-spun cottons that have been developed especially for baby knits.

If you use more than one yarn in a project, choose yarns of the same fiber and weight. When you knit a swatch to check the gauge, be sure to sample all the yarns you'll be using. Yarns from different manufacturers may differ in the way they knit up, hold their shape, or wash. Always launder a mixed-yarn item according to the directions for the most delicate yarn used. For example, you may be able to combine a mohair or lamb's wool with a washable wool of the same weight, but this blanket will need to be hand-washed, to protect the mohair or lamb's wool.

When you're looking for quality, as with most products, you'll find that you're likely to get what you pay for. Very inexpensive yarns may save you some money in the short run, but they often stretch easily and pill and, in general, don't hold up well. One of the reasons you knit is very likely for the pleasure of it, but when you're putting time and effort into a project, you'll want it to look good and last for a long time.

The Silver Lining

Worried about scratchy fibers irritating baby's sensitive skin? Unhappy with "floats" that show on the wrong side of multicolor blankets? Here's a way to kill two birds with one stone: Line the blanket after knitting it. Lining provides some extra warmth and can become an interesting design element, as well. Flannel, brushed cotton, cotton knit, and polar fleece are all good choices for lining baby blankets.

Before attaching the lining, block the knitted blanket and preshrink the lining material by washing it in hot water. Lay the blanket over the lining fabric and measure out 1 inch (2.5cm) beyond the blanket on all sides. Fold under a 1-inch (2.5cm) hem on all sides of the lining fabric; press. (You can skip this step if you use polar fleece.) Pin blanket and lining together, wrong sides facing, then stitch the lining in place by hand or machine stitching. To keep the blanket and lining from bagging, use quilting thread or strong yarn to tack the layers together at regular intervals, as you would with a quilt.

Be sure to buy enough yarn to complete your project. For instance, if a pattern calls for one skein of yarn packaged at 190 yards to a skein but you are substituting a yarn that is packaged in 100-yard skeins, you'll need to buy two skeins. Yardage is usually listed on the label; if not, ask your yarn shop personnel to check the manufacturer's specifications.

It's always a good idea to buy an extra skein or two to avoid running short. If you have to return for more yarn, you may find that the shop is either out of it or that what it has is from a different dye lot, which means the colors may be slightly, but noticeably, different. Some shops will set aside an additional skein for up to a month, just in case you need another; most shops will also accept unused skeins for cash or credit.

Yarns come in both circular and pull-out skeins. Circular skeins must be wound into balls before use. When you're using pull-out skeins, take the yarn from the inside for a smoother feed.

Tools of the Trade

Most knitters have strong preferences when it comes to selecting knitting needles, and the wide variety of choices can be confusing until you try them. Coated aluminum needles are durable but sometimes heavy in larger sizes. I find that some yarns tend to slip right off metal needles. Plastic or similar materials are lighter, though they can bend or break, and yarn sometimes sticks to

them. Bamboo needles have become my favorite. The yarn moves smoothly along them, even in hot, sticky weather, and they're quiet and comfortable to use.

After you've decided on the material you like best, you'll discover you also must choose among straight, double-point, and circular needles. Sometimes the project dictates what is needed. For instance, anything knit in a tube, like a hat or sock, is usually knitted on circular or double-point needles. If your project is rather wide, however, and has a lot of stitches, which is the case with some blanket patterns, you may find it easier to work with circular needles than with straight ones. If you try to force too many stitches onto a straight needle, the work bunches up, gets hard to move along, and is difficult to see. To knit flat work on circular needles, turn your work after each row, rather than knitting continuously around. Circular needles come in different lengths and have a flexible nylon or plastic center.

For smaller projects, straight needles will be fine. You'll also need double-point needles to knit the three-dimensional shapes featured on some of the patterns in this book. A set of crochet hooks is ideal for picking up dropped stitches, weaving in ends, and finishing some edges. (For information about picking up dropped stitches, see Easy Pickup, page 14.)

Needles come in numbered sizes. It's important to note whether the size is US, UK, or metric

— they're all different! The chart below gives equivalent sizes for all three. You'll note that in the US system, 0 is very small, whereas in the UK system, 0 is large. This book provides US and metric sizes in all the instructions.

Needle Conversion Chart

US	Metric	UK
0	2mm	14
1	2.25mm	13
	2.5mm	
2	2.75mm	12
	3mm	11
3	3.25mm	10
4	3.5mm	
5	3.75mm	9
6	4mm	8
7	4.5mm	7
8	5mm	6
9	5.5mm	5
10	6mm	4
10½	6.5mm	3
	7mm	2
	7.5mm	1
11	8mm	0
13	9mm	00
15	10mm	000

It's in the Bag

Depending on the project you are knitting, you don't need to purchase all of these items at once. But a well-supplied knitting bag, like all tool kits, makes life easier in many ways.

- Sets of needles, including straight, double-point, and circular
- Crochet hooks in small, medium, and large sizes, for picking up dropped stitches and finishing some edges
- 6-inch metal ruler with a needle gauge (a line of graduated holes that measure the needle diameter)
- Retractable tape measure
- Rubber covers or small corks to protect your needle points and to keep the stitches from falling off when you're not knitting
- Assortment of blunt-pointed tapestry needles
- T-shaped pins
- Small, sharp scissors
- Stitch holders (or safety pins for small numbers of stitches)
- Stitch markers, both round and split
- Cable needles
- Yarn bobbins, for small amounts of yarn when knitting intarsia patterns
- Removable adhesive notepads for marking your place in the directions
- Nice knitting bag

A Measured Approach

If you know that with the yarn and needles you're using 5 stitches and 7 rows equals 1 inch, you can make anything and guess what — it's the right size. Always calculate gauge over 4 inches (10cm). That's because counting stitches over 1 inch (2.5cm) can be misleading if your stitches are uneven or amount to a fraction. Here's an example of how to knit a swatch and figure out gauge:

1. If a pattern lists gauge as 16 stitches = 4 inches on size 7 needles, use size 7 needles to cast on 20 stitches (this is the number of gauge stitches, plus a few extra so that you don't need to measure the edge stitches, which may be uneven or draw in).
2. Following the stitch pattern you'll be using for the main part of your project (unless the pattern indicates otherwise), knit a swatch about 5 inches long. Do not block the swatch.
3. Lay the swatch on a firm, flat surface. Take care not to stretch the swatch, and make sure the side edges are uncurled. Lay a flat ruler from one side of the swatch to the other. Count the number of stitches within 4 inches (10cm). There should be exactly 16.
4. *If your swatch contains more* than 16 stitches in 4 inches, use larger needles and knit another swatch. Repeat steps 1 through 3.

    If your swatch contains fewer than 16 stitches in 4 inches, use smaller needles and knit another swatch. Repeat steps 1 through 3.
5. Even after you have established what needle size and yarn will get you to the right gauge, when you have knitted a few inches into the project, check again to make sure your gauge is holding true.

NOTE: Always use fresh yarn to check your gauge. Used yarn may be stretched and thus give an in-

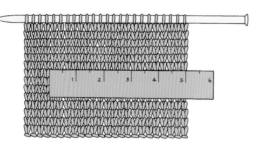

Measuring gauge

What Kind of Blanket?

Here are some rules of thumb for blanket dimensions, according to use:

Receiving Blanket	28" x 28" *to* 32" x 32"
Crib Blanket	30" x 36" *to* 36" x 45"
Throw/Afghan	48" x 60"
Carriage Blanket	30" x 36"

accurate measurement. Also, two needle sizes are sometimes specified for a pattern. If you change your larger-size needles to obtain the correct stitch gauge, adjust the size of the smaller needles to correspond.

Casting On

Casting on with a long-tail cast on makes an especially neat, firm, but elastic edge. If you tend to cast on tightly, you may want to switch to one needle size larger for this part.

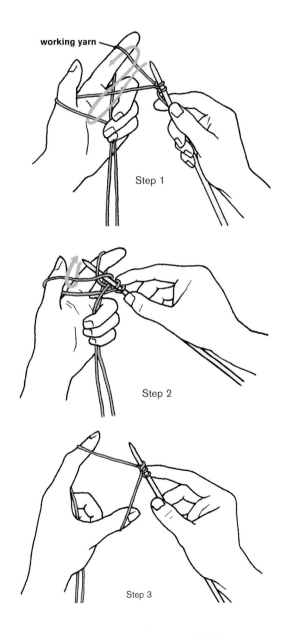

working yarn

Step 1

Step 2

Step 3

1. Estimate how long to make the "tail" by wrapping the yarn around the needle one time for each cast-on stitch you need, then adding a few extra inches. Make a slip knot right here, and slide the knot over a single knitting needle. Hold that needle in your right hand; hold the tail and the working end of the yarn in your left hand as shown. Insert needle through front loop of working yarn loop on your thumb. Wrap tail from back to front around needle.

2. Use the needle to draw the tail through the loop on your thumb.

3. Release the loop on your thumb, place your thumb underneath the working thread, and draw both toward you while holding the working thread and tail firmly in your fingers.

Casting Off

Casting off is sometimes called binding off. If you tend to cast off tightly, you may want to switch to one needle size larger. The simplest way to cast off is to knit two stitches to the right-hand needle, then draw the first one over the second. Don't pull too tightly, or your edge will be puckered and inelastic. When you reach the last stitch, pull the working end through the stitch and weave it into the inside.

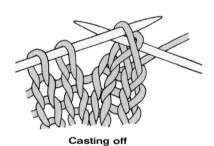

Casting off

Three-needle castoff is a useful technique if you want to cast off and at the same time join two pieces in an invisible seam. The two pieces must have an equal number of "live" stitches on needles. If you are using straight, single-pointed needles, make sure the needles are pointing in the same direction. Bring the two pieces (or two halves) together with the *right sides* facing.

1. With a third needle, beginning at the outer edge, insert the needle through the first stitch on the front and back needles and knit them together (see drawing).
2. Make a second stitch in the same way.

Keeping Safety in Mind

• Don't knit blankets (or other items) with long tassels or ribbons that might get wrapped around a baby's neck.

• Small items, such as buttons and beads, can come off and pose a choking hazard. If you do use sewn-on decorative items, make sure they are secured tightly with button thread and cannot be pulled off or loosen over time. Check the items every time the blanket is washed.

• Securely weave all yarn ends into the back of the knitted fabric. Yarn ends and long floats can become twisted around small wrists, fingers, and toes, cutting off circulation.

3. Pass the first stitch over the second one.
4. Continue casting off.

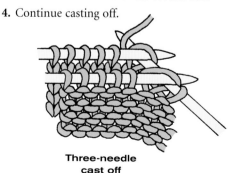

Three-needle cast off

On the Decrease

Decreasing can become an interesting design element in your project, and the pattern directions will specify which method to use. There are three common techniques. Because the first two (ssk and psso) result in a finished stitch that slants to the left, they are often used at the right side of an item; the last method (K2tog) results in a right-slanting stitch and so is used on the left edge.

SSK

The first method is called "ssk" (slip, slip, knit the two slipped stitches together). Slip two stitches, one at a time, from your left needle to your right, as if to knit. Then, slide the left needle from left to right through the front loops of the slipped stitches, and knit the two stitches together from this position. This technique makes a finished stitch that slants to the left on the finished side and is often used at the beginning of a row.

PSSO

To "psso" (pass slip stitch over knit stitch), slip one stitch from left to right needle, inserting needle as if to knit the stitch but without knitting it. Knit the next stitch, then draw the slipped stitch over the just-knitted stitch. The finished stitch will slant to the left on the finished side.

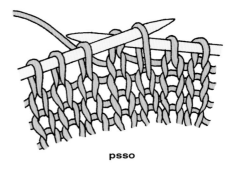

psso

K2TOG

For a finished stitch that slants to the right on the finished side, simply knit two stitches together by inserting the needle into both loops, just as you would to knit. K2tog (knit 2 together) is generally used at the end of a row.

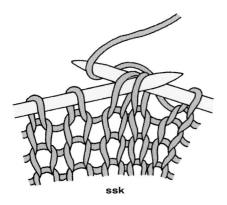

ssk

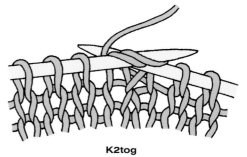

K2tog

Easy Pickup

Beginning knitters often panic when they drop a stitch. It's empowering to discover how easy it is to pick up dropped or half-made stitches. And this is why you need to include a crochet hook in your knitting bag! Working on the right side of stockinette stitch, find the last loop that's still knitted and insert the crochet hook from front to back. (On the wrong side, insert the needle from back to front.) Pull the loop just above the bar between the adjacent stitches, catch the bar with your hook, and draw it through the loop. If you have to pick up a number of stitches, take care to pick up the bars in the correct order.

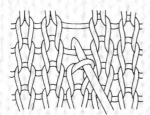

Picking up a dropped stitch knitwise

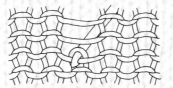

Picking up a dropped stitch purlwise

On the Increase

Increases allow you to shape your knitting as you work, and are often important design elements. It's helpful to learn a variety of techniques so that you can pick and choose whatever is appropriate for your needs. The illustrations that follow show three increase methods: bar increase, make 1 with a right slant, and make 1 with a left slant.

BAR INCREASE

The bar increase is a tight increase that leaves no hole, but shows as a short, horizontal bar on the right side of the fabric. Make it by knitting into the front of the loop in the usual way, but do not remove the stitch from the needle. Instead, knit into the back of the same stitch and slip both new stitches onto the right needle. To make this increase in stockinette stitch on wrong-side rows, purl into the front and then the back of the stitch before removing it from the needle.

For a bar increase of two stitches, work into the front loop, the back loop, and the front loop again before taking the three new stitches off the needle.

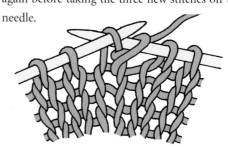

Bar increase

MAKE 1, RIGHT SLANT

1. Look for the horizontal bar between the first stitch on your left-hand needle and the last stitch on your right-hand needle. With the tip of your left needle, pick up this bar from back to front.

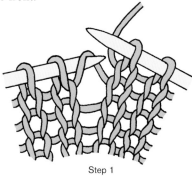

Step 1

2. Knit into the bar from the front, which twists the new stitch and gives it a slant to the right. Even though it may seem a bit difficult to get your needle into the bar from front to back, it's important to do so in order to avoid creating a small hole in the fabric.

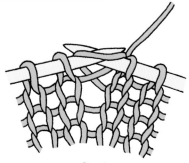

Step 2

MAKE 1, LEFT SLANT

1. Pick up the bar from front to back.

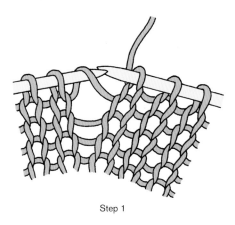

Step 1

2. Knit into the back of the bar, which twists the new stitch to the left.

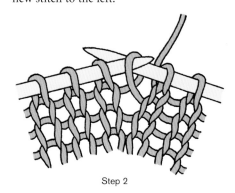

Step 2

NOTE: To make 1 at the end of a round, pick up the horizontal strand between the last and the first stitches of the round.

Around We Go

Some projects have three-dimensional shapes that require knitting in the round. To make stockinette stitch when you knit in the round, you always knit on the right side, continuing around the circular or double-point needles without ever turning your work. (On straight needles, stockinette is created by knitting on one side, turning, and purling on the return.) For small items, use double-point needles to knit in the round; for larger tubes, use circular needles. Except for occasional decorative details and the felted blanket on page 98, blankets aren't knitted in the round to create tubes. However, several blankets in this book are knitted from the center out on double-point and then circular needles, with increases at the corners to enlarge the dimensions. You'll need to practice some basic knitting-in-the-round techniques to work on these projects.

To knit with double-point needles, cast on the correct number of stitches for your project and divide the stitches evenly among three of the needles (or as the pattern directs). Lay the work on a flat surface, forming the three needles into a triangle. Arrange the cast-on stitches so they are flat and all facing toward the center of the triangle. Look carefully along the needles and especially at the corners to make sure that the stitches don't take an extra twist around the needle.

Double-Point Tips

- To avoid the common problem of loose stitches that develop where the needles change, make sure that each time you reach those corners you snug the yarn firmly after knitting the first stitch on the new needle. Another trick to keep the tension even is to move several stitches from one needle to the next after the first few rounds.

- To make it easier to handle your knitting, arrange your needles so the ends of the two you are working with lie on top of the third needle.

- Use a stitch marker, small safety pin, or piece of yarn in a different color to mark the first stitch of the round.

- Make sure that you never reverse directions when knitting in the round.

The next step is the trickiest: Carefully lift the needles, keeping the stitches aligned, and use the working yarn that formed the last cast-on stitch to knit the first stitch on the left-hand needle. Snug the yarn firmly before knitting the

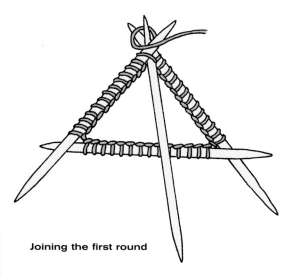

Joining the first round

second stitch. (Do not tie to join.) Knit across until the left-hand needle is empty. Use the empty needle to knit the stitches on the next needle. Continue knitting until the first round is complete. Place a marker on the needle to indicate the beginning of each new round.

To knit with circular needles, cast on the correct number of stitches as usual, then lay the work on a flat surface. Arrange the stitches facing the center of the circle and carefully knit the first couple of stitches on the left-hand needle, taking care not to twist any stitches around the needles. Snug the yarn tightly between the last cast-on stitch and the first stitch in the first round. (Do not tie to join.) Place a marker between these two stitches to help you keep track of rounds.

Joining New Yarn

When you run out of yarn and need to start a new end, do so toward the edge of the blanket, where the join is less likely to be noticed. You may be able to overlap the new yarn with the old and knit the two together for three or four stitches before dropping the old yarn. (See drawing below.) When you come to those doubled stitches in the next row, be sure to knit the two yarns together as one. Be aware that if your yarn is very smooth, this join may show. Do not use this method when changing colors.

A more invisible method is to lay the new end along the back of the work and carry it forward for six or seven stitches by weaving the working yarn over and under it in much the same way that you handle a second color yarn in multicolor knitting. Once it is snugly woven in this manner, you can simply pick it up and begin knitting with it. At this point, weave in the tail end of the old yarn in the same manner. If you follow this procedure faithfully throughout a project, you will have few, if any, ends to darn in at the end — and you'll thank yourself heartily for that!

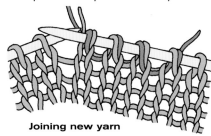

Joining new yarn

Colorful Effects

You can create an infinite number of fascinating designs by knitting with two or more colors in a single row or round. You'll encounter two kinds of multicolor knitting in this book: Fair Isle (also called stranded knitting) and intarsia. Which method to use depends on the nature of the pattern. If the two (or more) colors interchange regularly all the way across the row, with no more than about eight stitches of any one color used successively, Fair Isle knitting is most convenient. When a color pattern is isolated in a field of another color, distant from other repeats, or it is used only once, then intarsia is the way to go. (You may also use duplicate stitch, instead of intarsia, in some instances. See page 88.) In this book, we illustrate the sequence of multicolor knitting in charts that are color-matched to the photos of the finished projects. When you follow a chart using either Fair Isle or intarsia, you usually start at the bottom right corner, then follow along from right to left when working on the right side of the piece, and from left to right when working on the wrong side.

FAIR ISLE KNITTING

Developing certain habits will help you avoid both tangles and tears with Fair Isle knitting. When you change colors, always take the color you want to emphasize from below the other. On the front, the color handled this way will dominate the pattern

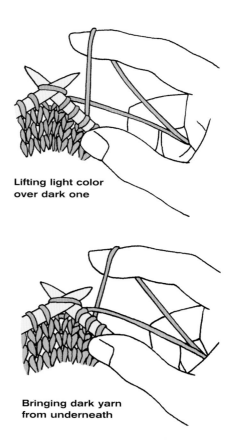

Lifting light color over dark one

Bringing dark yarn from underneath

and create a more uniform design. Be sure to be consistent and take the same yarn over and the other under throughout the project.

If you are able to use one hand for one color and the other hand for a second color, you'll find that two-color knitting goes quickly and easily. Keep the second color pulled firmly over the index finger of your left hand, as you would hold yarn for crocheting. When you are not using the second color, move your finger forward for one stitch and backward for the next so that the yarn weaves neatly along the back of the work.

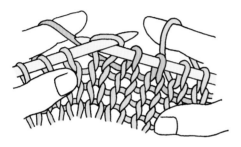

Two-handed color knitting

When you knit with more than one color, carry the other color or colors along on the wrong side, keeping the carried yarn loose so that it doesn't pucker the fabric. Don't carry the yarn for more than three stitches or you'll end up with long loops that can get snagged by baby's tiny and curious fingers. To avoid this, catch the carried yarn by wrapping the working yarn from beneath and around it every three or four stitches.

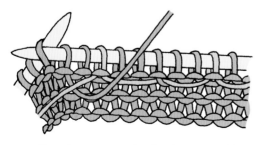

Carrying a second color (wrong side)

INTARSIA

To prepare for intarsia knitting, wind several bobbins or "butterflies" (see drawing, facing page; tie one yarn end loosely around the bundle and draw out the other end, as needed) with yarns of all the colors you'll be using. These will allow you to feed the yarn gradually and are less likely to tangle than if you use whole skeins. (Some knitters prefer to simply let long lengths of each yarn

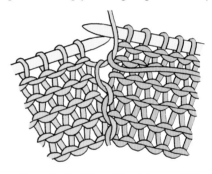

Intarsia knitting: Step 1 (wrong side)

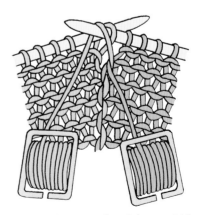

Intarsia knitting: Step 2 (wrong side)

color hang from the back of their work and comb them loose when they intertwine.)

When you begin each new color, leave the old color behind and knit with the new color as indicated in the directions or on the accompanying chart. Be sure to wrap the old and new yarns around each other as shown in the drawings on page 20. This locks the yarns neatly together and creates a strong, smooth join with no gaps in the work. Be sure to do this interlock on the wrong side of the work on both knit and purl rows.

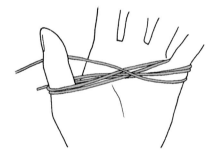

Winding a butterfly skein

Blocking Your Work

You may be anxious to see your beautiful new creation tucked around baby, but do take the time to weave in any loose ends you missed on the wrong side of the fabric, then block it properly. You'll be surprised at how unevenness disappears when you block your knitting.

You can steam-block all-wool fabrics by holding a steam iron just above the surface so the steam penetrates the fabric, or cover the surface with a wet pressing cloth and lightly touch the iron to it. Either way, avoid pressing hard or moving the iron back and forth. Never iron or block a ribbed hem; it will lose its elasticity.

For wool blends, mohair, angora, alpaca, or cashmere, just dampen the knitted piece by spraying it lightly with water, then pin it to a flat surface where you can safely leave it to air-dry. Be sure to pin it so that the facing edges measure the same, the corners are right angles, and the stitches line up straight. Do not block blankets knitted with chenille or ribbon yarns.

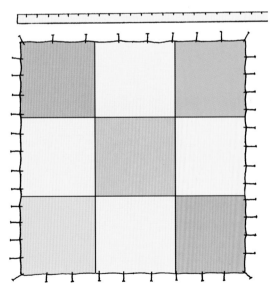

Blocking a finished blanket

Aran Blanket

Designed by Linda Daniels, Northampton Wools

In the famous fisherman's sweaters of the Aran Islands, the moss stitch represents seaweed and the cables represent the fisherman's rope. For the baby sleeping under this blanket, they just mean comfort and warmth. Cable knitting offers many textural variations, and you'll find two versions — a wide plait and a narrow cable — in this pattern. If you've never tried the cable technique, you'll find that once you get the hang of using the cable needle, it's simpler than it looks — and fun.

Finished measurements: 34" by 40" (86.5cm by 101.5cm)

Yarn: Jaeger Matchmaker Merino Aran, 100% wool, machine-washable, aran weight, 1200 yds (1080m) cream

Needles

One #8 (5.0mm) circular needle, 24" (61cm) long, *or size needed to obtain gauge*

One cable needle

Gauge: 20 sts = 4" (10cm) on #8 (5.0mm) needles in St st

Other supplies: Row counter, yarn needle, 14 stitch markers

NOTE: All the patterns in this blanket are worked in repeating blocks of 8 rows each. Use a row counter to help you keep track of where you are in the pattern.

---

cn = cable needle ◆ **K** = knit ◆ **P** = purl
sl = slip ◆ **st(s)** = stitch(es) ◆ **St st** = stockinette stitch ◆ **yd(s)** = yard(s)

Aran Stitches

Seed Stitch (multiple of 2 sts)

Rows 1, 3, 5, and 7: *K1, P1; repeat from *.
Rows 2, 4, 6, and 8: *P1, K1; repeat from *.

Seed stitch

Double Moss Stitch (multiple of 4 sts + 2)

Rows 1, 4, 5, and 8: K2, *P2, K2;
repeat from *.
Rows 2, 3, 6, and 7: P2, *K2, P2;
repeat from *.

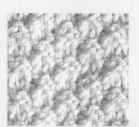

Double moss stitch

Wide Plait Cable (14 sts)

Row 1: P5, sl 2 to cn and hold in back, K2,
K2 from cn, P5.
Row 2: K5, P4, K5.
Row 3: P4, sl 1 to cn and hold in back, K2,
K1 from cn, sl 2 to cn and hold in front, K1,
K2 from cn, P4.
Row 4: K4, P2, K2, P2, K4.
Row 5: P3, sl 1 to cn and hold in back, K2,
K1 from cn, P2, sl 2 to cn and hold in front,
K1, K2 from cn, P3.
Row 6: K3, P2, K4, P2, K3.
Row 7: P2, sl 1 to cn and hold in back, K2,
K1 from cn, P4, sl 2 to cn and hold in front,
K1, K2 from cn, P2.
Row 8: K2, P2, K6, P2, K2.

Wide plait cable

Narrow Cable (10 sts)

Rows 1, 5, and 7: P2, K6, P2.
Rows 2, 4, 6, and 8: K2, P6, K2.
Row 3: P2, sl 3 to cn and hold in back, K3,
K3 from cn, P2.

Narrow cable

KNITTING THE BOTTOM BORDER

With the #8 (5.0mm) needle, cast on 174 sts.

Rows 1–8: Work in seed st to end of each row.

KNITTING THE BLANKET

Row 1 sets up the patterns. Place stitch markers before and after pattern groups. Work on the right side.

Work 8 sts seed stitch (place st marker).

Work 10 sts double moss stitch (place st marker).

Work narrow cable (place st marker), work wide plait cable, work narrow cable.

Work 18 sts double moss stitch (place st marker).

Work narrow cable, work wide plait cable, work narrow cable (place st marker).

Work 18 sts double moss stitch (place st marker).

Work narrow cable, work wide plait cable, work narrow cable (place st marker).

Work 10 sts double moss stitch (place st marker).

Work 8 sts seed stitch.

Repeat the blocks of 8 rows of each pattern as established, until the blanket measures approximately 39" (99cm). End after Row 8 of pattern.

KNITTING THE TOP BORDER

Rows 1–8: Work in seed stitch to end of each row.

Cast off loosely. Weave in all yarn ends.

Working a Cable

To make a cable, place the number of stitches specified in the pattern on a third needle and hold them either behind or in front of the knitted piece, as directed. Work the next stitches on your left-hand needle according to the pattern, then work the stitches from the cable needle. Take care not to twist stitches.

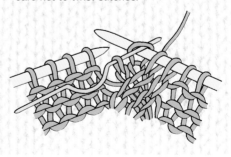

Baby Bunting

Designed by Louise Silverman, Sakonnet Purls

It's easy to bundle a baby into this traditional bunting when you go out on a cold morning. The bunting covers everything from head to toes, and it has optional slits in front and back so you can run the car-seat strap through without scrunching up the bottom of the bunting. Thoughtful details, like the honeycomb pattern on the placket and back and the con-trasting-color garter stitch stripes on the front and sleeves, give this garment a touch of elegance.

Size and finished measurements:
Infant (3–6 months), 16" (40.5cm) wide, 24" (61cm) from shoulders to toes

Yarn: Brown Sheep Lamb's Pride Superwash, 100% wool, bulky weight

600 yds (540m) mc (Amethyst)

6 yds (5m) cc A (Sweeten Pink)

30 yds (27m) cc B (Red Wing)

Needles

One set #7 (4.5mm) straight needles

One set #10½ (6.5mm) straight needles, *or size needed to obtain gauge*

One #9 (5.5mm) circular needle, 24" (61cm) long

Gauge: 14 sts = 4" (10cm) on #10.5 (6.5mm) needles in St st

Other supplies: Five ¾" buttons, 2 stitch holders

---

cc = contrasting color ◆ **inc** = increase
HP = honeycomb pattern ◆ **K** = knit
K2tog = knit 2 stitches together ◆ **mc** = main color ◆ **P** = purl ◆ **sl** = slip
ssk = slip, slip, knit the 2 slipped stitches together ◆ **st(s)** = stitch(es) ◆ **St st** = stockinette stitch

Honeycomb Pattern

(4 sts, repeats every 4 rows)

To knit the Honeycomb Pattern (HP), follow these directions:

Row 1: Knit second st but do not take it off the needle (step 1 below), knit first st, then sl both sts off the needle together (step 2 below). Knit fourth st through back but do not take it off the needle (step 3 below), knit third st, sl both sts off the needle together (step 4 below).

Rows 2 and 4: Purl to end of each row.

Row 3: Knit second st through back but do not take it off the needle, knit first st, then sl both sts off the needle together. K fourth st but do not take it off the needle, knit third st, then sl both sts off the needle together.

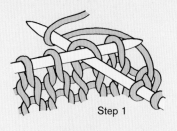

Step 1

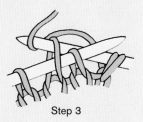

Step 3

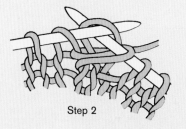

Step 2

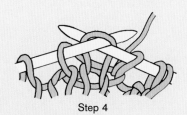

Step 4

KNITTING THE BACK

With #10½ (6.5mm) needles and mc, cast on 54 sts.

Row 1: Inc 1, K5, P1, work 4 sts in Honeycomb Pattern (HP; see facing page), P1, K30, P1, work 4 sts in Honeycomb Pattern (HP), P1, K4, inc 1, K1. You will have 56 sts.

Row 2: P7, K1, HP, K1, P30, K1, HP, K1, P7.

Row 3: Inc 1, K6, P1, HP, P1, K30, P1, HP, P1, K5, inc 1, K1. You will have 58 sts.

Row 4: P8, K1, HP, K1, P30, K1, HP, K1, P8.

Continue with the pattern as established, increasing 2 sts in each odd-numbered row until you have 64 sts.

Work even in the same pattern until the piece measures 3.5" (9cm).

Next right-side row: Ssk, work in pattern until last 2 sts, K2tog. You will have 62 sts.

Work even in the same pattern until the piece measures 6" (15cm).

Next right-side row: Ssk, work in pattern until last 2 sts, K2tog. You will have 60 sts.

MAKING THE CAR-SEAT SLIT

NOTE: If you choose not to make the car-seat slit, ignore the instructions in this section for the garter stitch border and the cast-off for the slit, but continue in established pattern, making decreases at the beginning and end of the row as before when piece measures 9" (28cm). To make the flaps for the slit, see page 31.

Work even in the same pattern until the piece measures 7" (18cm).

To make the garter stitch border for the car-seat slit, on the next 3 *wrong-side* rows, P25 sts, K10 sts, P25 sts.

Next right-side row: Cast off center 6 sts to make the car-seat slit.

Next wrong-side row: Work in established pattern to opening; K2tog, K4, K2tog from car-seat flap sts on holder; continue pattern for remainder of row.

Next right-side row: Ssk, work in pattern until last 2 sts, K2tog. You will have 58 sts.

To complete the border for the car-seat slit, on the next 2 *wrong-side rows*, P24 sts, K10 sts, P24 sts.

Work even in the pattern until the piece measures 11" (28cm).

Next right-side row: Ssk, work in pattern until last 2 sts, K2tog. You will have 56 sts.

Work even in the pattern until the piece measures 19" (48cm).

Next two rows: At the beginning of each row, cast off 1 st for armhole markers. You will have 54 sts.

Work even in the pattern until the armhole measures 5" (12.5cm).

Next row: Work 18 sts in pattern, cast off center 18 sts for neck, work in pattern to end of row.

Next two rows, cast off remaining sts for the shoulders, starting from the outside.

KNITTING THE FRONT

With the #10½ (6.5mm) needles and mc, cast on 54 sts. Work the same as the back until you finish the garter st ridges above the car-seat slit. At this point you have 58 sts.

Next row: Cast off center 2 sts for placket opening. You will have 56 sts, 28 sts on each side.

Continue working both sides separately the same as the back until the piece measures 21" (53cm). At this point, you will have 52 sts, 26 sts on each side.

Next two rows: Cast off 3 sts at each neck edge. You will have 46 sts, 23 sts on each side.

Next two rows: Cast off 2 sts at neck edge. You will have 42 sts, 21 sts on each side.

Next six rows: Cast off 1 st at neck edge. You will have 36 sts, 18 sts on each side.

Continue working even until the front measures the same as the back.

Next two rows: Cast off remaining sts for the shoulders, starting from the outside.

KNITTING THE SLEEVES

NOTE: Instructions given are for one sleeve. Make two identical sleeves.

With the #10½ (6.5mm) needles and mc, pick up and knit 38 sts around the armhole.

Row 1: Purl.

Row 2: Knit.

Continue working in St st until sleeve measures 1.5" (4cm).

Car-Seat Opening

This little flapped opening is handy for strapping a bundled baby into a car seat. The slit is knit into both the front and the back, and a small interior flap prevents cold air from seeping through the opening. The garter stitch surround lends a decorative touch and could be knit in one of the contrasting colors. Or knit it in plain stockinette, so it blends into the rest of the knitting.

Making the Car-Seat Flap

The car-seat slits, and the flaps that attach to them, are optional. These instructions are for one flap; you'll need two identical flaps.

With the #10½ (6.5mm) needles and mc, cast on 8 sts.
Rows 1–10: Knit to the end of each row.
Place stitches on holders.

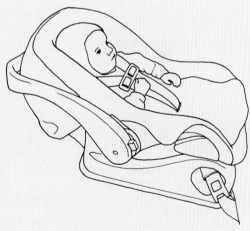

Next row: Ssk, knit to last 2 sts, K2tog. You will have 36 sts.

Continue working in St st until sleeve measures 2¾" (7cm).

Next right-side row: Ssk, knit to last 2 sts, K2tog. You will have 34 sts.

Continue working in St st until sleeve measures 4" (10cm).

Next right-side row: Ssk, knit to last 2 sts, K2tog. You will have 32 sts.

Continue working in St st until sleeve measures 5½" (14cm).

Next right-side row: Change to cc B and work 4 rows in garter st (knit each row).

Next row: Change to cc A and knit 2 rows in garter st.

Next row: Change to mc and knit to the end of the row.

Next row: K2tog; *K2tog, K1; repeat from * to last 4 sts; K2tog, K2tog. You will have 20 sts.

Next row: Change to the #7 (4.5mm) needles and work in K1, P1 ribbing for 2.5" (6.5cm). Cast off loosely.

KNITTING THE HOOD

With the #10½ (6.5mm) needles and mc, cast on 60 sts.

Row 1: Knit.

Row 2: Purl.

Work even in St st until the hood measures 1½" (4cm).

Next row: Inc 1, knit to last 2 sts, inc 1, K1. You will have 62 sts.

Work even in St st until the hood measures 3" (7.5cm).

Next row: Inc 1, knit to last 2 sts, inc 1, K1. You will have 64 sts.

Work even in St st until the hood measures 4½" (11.25cm).

Next row: Inc 1, knit to last 2 sts, inc 1, K1. You will have 66 sts.

Work even in St st until the hood measures 6¼" (15.6cm).

Next row: K5, *K2tog, K9; repeat from * to last 6 sts; K2tog, K4. You will have 60 sts. Leave these sts on a stitch holder.

ASSEMBLING THE BUNTING

Sew the front to the back at the shoulders, with the right sides together.

Fold the hood in half, right sides together, and sew along the cast-on row to form the top seam.

Sew the sides of the hood to the neck, leaving the sts on the holder for the hood opening.

KNITTING THE PLACKET

With the #9 (5.5mm) circular needle and cc A, starting at the bottom of the opening of the right front, pick up and knit:

60 sts along the right placket opening

60 sts around the hood

60 sts along the left placket opening. You will have 180 sts.

Row 1: Knit.

Row 2: Change to cc B and knit to the end of the row.

Row 3: Knit.

Mark locations of the buttonholes with pins. There should be five buttonholes evenly spaced along the right side of the placket, with the first buttonhole 1" (2.5cm) from the bottom of the opening and the last buttonhole 1" (2.5cm) below the neck opening.

Row 4: Knit to end of row, casting off 1 st for each buttonhole.

Row 5: Knit to end of row, casting on 1 st in the place of each cast-off st.

Row 6: Knit to end of row. Cast off with medium tension.

FINISHING UP

Sew the side and sleeve seams, and baste the car-seat flaps to the inside of the bunting. Cut the yarn and weave in all the ends. Sew on the buttons.

Corner-to-Corner Blanket

Traditional design, adapted by Gwen Steege

Babies love to be safely snug in a cozy cocoon of a blanket. Because it's knitted from corner to corner in a stretchy garter stitch, this especially easy-to-knit receiving blanket combines the perfect amount of security with a surprising amount of give. It's fun to knit, starting with just one stitch. A simple "yarn over" provides both shaping and decoration — and couldn't be easier! This blanket can be knit in two different yarns — a sport-weight washable merino wool (pictured) and a worsted-weight cotton.

Finished measurements: 30" (76cm) square

Sport-Weight Yarn (pictured):
Gem's 100% pure merino washable wool
730 yds (657m) (raspberry)
Needles for sport-weight yarn: One #4 (3.5mm) circular needle, 24" (61cm) long, *or size needed to obtain gauge*
Gauge for sport-weight wool: 22 sts = 4" (10cm) on #4 (3.5mm) needles in garter st

Worsted-Weight Yarn:
Bernat's Cottontots, 645 yds (580m)
Needles for worsted-weight yarn: One #7 (4.5mm) circular needle, 24" (61cm) long, *or size needed to obtain gauge*
Gauge for worsted-weight yarn: 20 sts = 4" (10cm) on #7 (4.5mm) needles in garter st

Other supplies: Yarn needle

K = knit ◆ **K2tog** = knit 2 stitches together
P = purl ◆ **st(s)** = stitch(es) ◆ **YO** = yarn over

Project Linus

Begun in 1995, Project Linus is a volunteer, nonprofit organization whose mission is to provide "love, a sense of security, warmth and comfort to children who are seriously ill, traumatized, or otherwise in need through the gifts of new, homemade, washable blankets and afghans, lovingly created by volunteer blanketeers." All styles of blankets are welcome, including quilts, crocheted or knitted afghans, and receiving blankets. More than 400,000 blankets have been delivered to children around the world. This blanket is a favorite of the knitting volunteers. For information, including local chapters and patterns, visit their Web site at www.projectlinus.org; or contact them at Project Linus, P.O. Box 5621, Bloomington, IL 61702-5621; 309.664.7814.

INCREASING FROM THE BOTTOM CORNER	SPORT	WORSTED
Cast on 1 st. Turn after casting on and after each subsequent row.		
Row 1: Inc 1 by knitting into the front and back of the st. You will have	2 sts	2 sts
Rows 2–5: Inc 1 as above, knit to end of row. At the end of Row 5 you will have	6 sts	6 sts
Row 6: K3, YO, knit to the end of the row. You will have	7 sts	7 sts
Repeat Row 6, knitting the YO st from each previous row, until you have	190 sts	170 sts
DECREASING TOWARD THE TOP CORNER		
Row 1: K3, YO, K2tog, knit to the end of the row.		
Row 2: K3, YO, K2tog, knit to last 4 sts, K2tog, K2. You will have **NOTE:** When you knit 2 sts together at the end of the row, you are knitting together the YO from the previous row with one of the border stitches.	189 sts	169 sts
Repeat Row 2 until you have	6 sts	6 sts
Next row: K2, K2tog, K2. You will have	5 sts	5 sts
Next row: K2, K2tog, K1. You will have	4 sts	4 sts
Next row: K1, K2tog, K1. You will have	3 sts	3 sts
Next row: K1, K2tog. You will have	2 sts	2 sts
Next row: K2tog. Bind off the remaining st.		
Cut yarn and weave in the loose ends. Because this blanket stretches so much, it's important to leave tails of about 2" (5cm) to weave in, so the ends won't pull out.		

Safari Parade

Designed by Barbara Telford, Woodsmoke Woolworks

Giraffes, elephants, and ostriches parade around this blanket with such verve that you almost feel like you're on a safari. The blanket is made up of four identical triangles; it's knit in the round, from the center out, on double-pointed and circular needles. The color patterns are knit using the intarsia method (see pages 20–21). Although this is a complex color pattern, the stitch is straight stockinette.

Finished measurements: 39" (98cm) square

Yarn: Briggs & Little Regal, 100% wool, double-knit weight

272 yds (249m) mc (Dark Blue)

544 yds (498m) cc A (Light Blue)

544 yds (498m) cc B (Light Green)

272 yds (249m) cc C (Dark Green)

30 yds (27m) cc D (Bleached White)

100 yds (92m) cc E (Charcoal)

272 yds (249m) cc F (Gray)

272 yds (249m) cc G (Forest Brown)

272 yds (249m) cc H (Yellow)

Needles

Five #7 (4.5mm) circular needles, maximum length available, *or size needed to obtain gauge*

Set of five #7 (4.5mm) dp needles, *or same as above*

Gauge: 20 sts = 4" (10cm) on #7 (4.5mm) needles in St st

Other supplies: Yarn needle, stitch markers

---

cc = contrast color ◆ **cn** = cable needle ◆ **dp** = double pointed ◆ **inc** = increase
K = knit ◆ **mc** = main color ◆ **P** = purl ◆ **sl** = slip ◆ **st(s)** = stitch(es)
St st = stockinette stitch

With the #7 (4.5mm) dp needle and mc, cast on 4 sts. Refer to Center Charts A, B, and C (pages 41–43) for colors in this section. See also Colorful Effects, pages 19–21, and On the Increase, page 14.

Row 1: Inc 1 in each st purlwise. You will have 8 sts. (Center Charts, line 1)

Row 2: Inc 1 in each st knitwise. You will have 16 sts.

Row 3: *Inc 1 purlwise, P2, inc 1 purlwise; repeat from * to end of row. You will have 24 sts.

KNITTING IN THE ROUND

Distribute the 24 sts evenly among four dp needles (6 sts on each needle), and begin knitting in the round. The first stitch on each needle is the corner stitch. Note that the increase at the beginning of each row is in the stitch *following* the corner stitch. Work each corner stitch in the same color as the stitch adjacent to it. Center Charts A and B (pages 41–43) are repeated on each needle. The first 3 stitches on each needle are the stitches on line 3 of Center Chart A; the last 3 stitches are the stitches on line 3 of Center Chart B. (See also Safari Parade Layout, on page 47, for an overview of pattern placement.)

Round 1: Knit to end of rnd (Center Charts, line 4).

Round 2: Continuing to follow Center Charts, K1, inc 1 in next st, knit to last st, inc 1. You will have 8 sts on each needle.

Round 3: K1, inc 1 in next st, knit to last st, inc 1. You will have 10 sts on each needle.

Round 4: K1, inc 1 in next st, knit to last st, inc 1. You will have 12 sts on each needle.

Continuing to follow Center Charts, repeat Rounds 1–4, increasing at the beginning and end of each needle as established. Switch to four circular needles when necessary. When Center Charts A and B are completed (line 63, 96 sts per needle), begin line 64 of Edge Charts (pages 42–44) as follows: 5 stitches of Edge Chart C, 44 stitches of Edge Chart D, 44 stitches of Edge Chart E, and 3 stitches of Edge Chart F *on each needle*. Work charts and increases until you have 172 stitches on each needle (line 113 of Edge Charts).

Last two rounds: Work loosely in K1, P1 ribbing, continuing to inc at the beginning and end of each needle, as established.

Cast off in ribbing, knitting over purl sts and purling over knit sts.

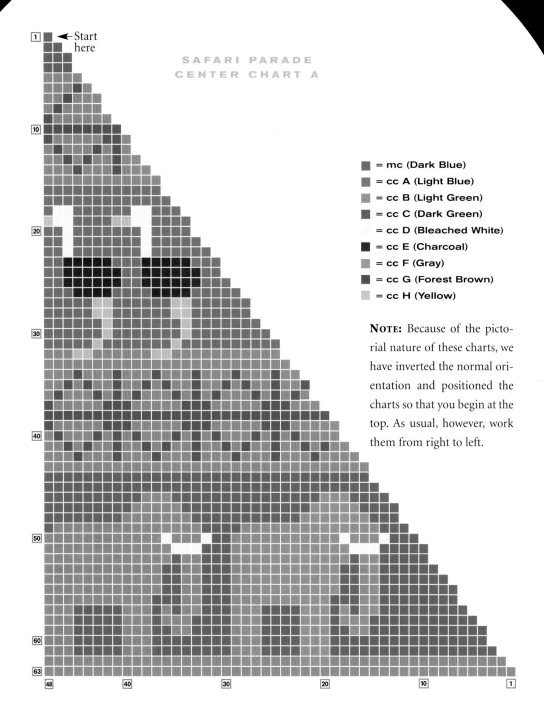

1 ←Start here

SAFARI PARADE
CENTER CHART A

■ = mc (Dark Blue)
■ = cc A (Light Blue)
■ = cc B (Light Green)
■ = cc C (Dark Green)
□ = cc D (Bleached White)
■ = cc E (Charcoal)
■ = cc F (Gray)
■ = cc G (Forest Brown)
■ = cc H (Yellow)

NOTE: Because of the pictorial nature of these charts, we have inverted the normal orientation and positioned the charts so that you begin at the top. As usual, however, work them from right to left.

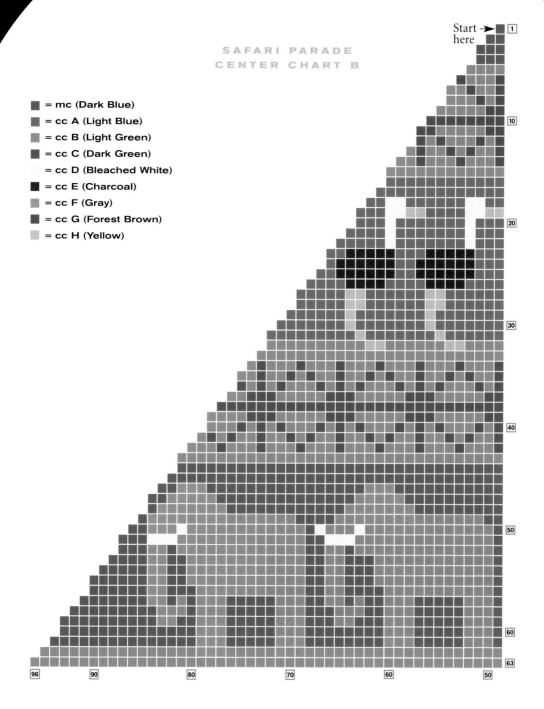

SAFARI PARADE
CENTER CHART B

Start → here

= mc (Dark Blue)
= cc A (Light Blue)
= cc B (Light Green)
= cc C (Dark Green)
= cc D (Bleached White)
= cc E (Charcoal)
= cc F (Gray)
= cc G (Forest Brown)
= cc H (Yellow)

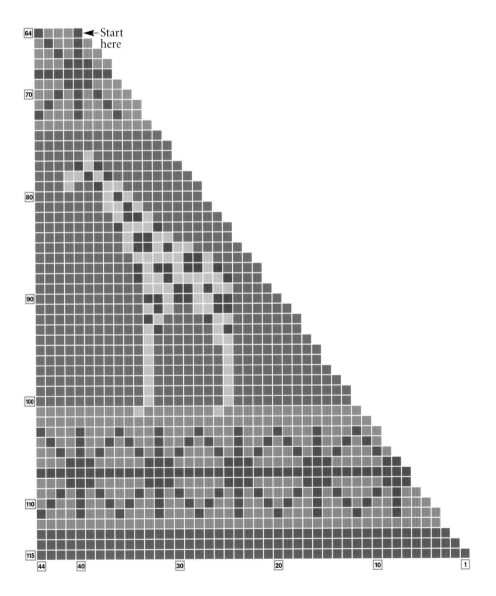

Start here

64
70
80
90
100
110
115

44 40 30 20 10 1

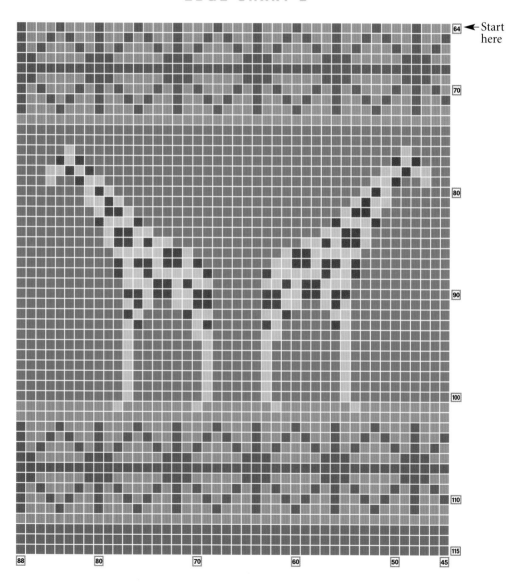

64 ←Start here

70

80

90

100

110

115

88   80   70   60   50   45

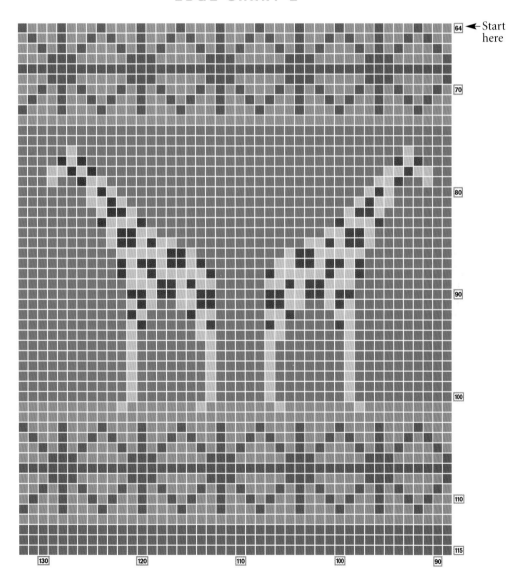

Start here

■ = mc (Dark Blue)
■ = cc A (Light Blue)
▨ = cc B (Light Green)
■ = cc C (Dark Green)
□ = cc D (Bleached White)
■ = cc E (Charcoal)
▨ = cc F (Gray)
■ = cc G (Forest Brown)
▨ = cc H (Yellow)

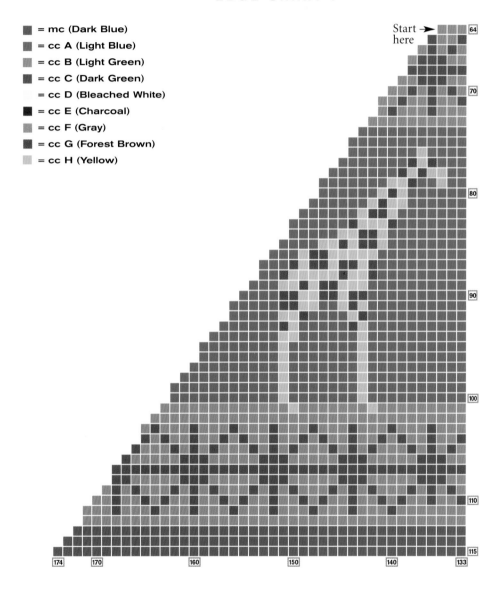

Start → here

64

70

80

90

100

110

115

174 170 160 150 140 133

C / F	D	E	F / C
E	A / B	B / A	D
D	A / B	B / A	E
C / F	E	D	F / C

Tumbling Blocks

Designed by Ruth Fresia, Williamstown, MA

Tumbling Blocks started as an Amish quilting pattern and has become a favorite knitting pattern as well. The blocks seem to be three dimensional and change their orientation as you look at them. You can make the Tumbling Blocks either by knitting each color section separately and joining them together or by knitting one row at a time in intarsia. The instructions given here are for the intarsia method, where you may be working with as many as 20 strands of yarn in a single row.

Finished measurements: 30" by 32" (75cm by 80cm)

Yarn: Brown Sheep Lamb's Pride Superwash, 100% wool, worsted weight

425 yds (382m) mc (Saffron)

225 yds (203m) cc A (Sapphire)

225 yds (203m) cc B (Serendipity Turquoise)

Needles: One #7 (4.5mm) circular needle, 29" (74cm) long, *or size needed to obtain gauge*

Gauge: 20 sts = 4" (10cm) on #7 (4.5mm) needles in St st

Other supplies: Yarn needle, 20 bobbins

---

dp = double pointed ◆ **K** = knit ◆ **P** = purl
RS = right side ◆ **sl** = slip ◆ **st(s)** = stitch(es) ◆ **St st** = stockinette stitch
WS = wrong side

With #7 (4.5mm) needle and mc, cast on 136 sts.

Rows 1–11: Sl 1, knit to end of needle (garter stitch). You will have 6 ridges after Row 11.

TUMBLING BLOCKS PATTERN

NOTE: An 8-stitch border of garter stitch (knit on right- and wrong-side rows) edges both sides of the blanket. The center Tumbling Blocks pattern is worked in stockinette stitch, following the chart on page 51. The pattern consists of six 20-stitch repeats across the blanket, and the 62 rows are repeated three times from top to bottom. Begin the chart at the bottom right and work from right to left on the right side. Be sure to take note that when you purl back on the wrong side, you must follow the chart from left to right. Work the color pattern using the intarsia technique, taking care to wrap the new yarn around the old yarn at each color change before leaving the old color behind. All wraps must be made at the back of the blanket. Before beginning the pattern, wind 8 bobbins or "butterfly" skeins with mc and 6 bobbins each with cc A and cc B. (For further information about intarsia knitting, see Colorful Effects, pages 19–21.)

Row 1 (RS): With mc, Sl 1, K7, K120 sts of the Tumbling Blocks chart (page 51), starting at line 1 at the bottom right-hand corner of the chart; with mc, K8.

Row 2 (WS): With mc, Sl 1, K7, P120 sts of line 2 of the chart, following the chart from left to right. Join bobbins filled with cc A at the points indicated, and switch to bobbins filled with mc after each color change. End with K8 in mc.

Row 3 (RS): Sl 1, K7, K120 sts of line 3 of the chart, following the chart from right to left, and joining bobbins filled with cc B at the points indicated. End with K8 in mc.

Row 4 (WS): Sl 1, K7, P120 sts of line 4 of the chart, following the chart from left to right. End with K8 in mc.

Next rows: Continue to work 8 sts of mc at each border and to follow the chart until you have repeated the 62-row pattern three times.

KNITTING THE TOP BORDER

Row 198 (RS): With mc, sl 1, knit to end of row.

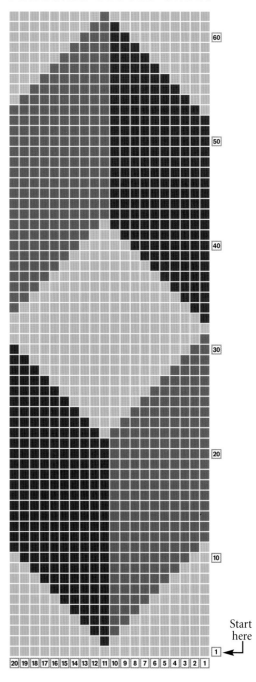

Rows 199–208: Sl 1, knit to end of row.
You will have 6 ridges after Row 208.

Cast off all sts and weave ends into back
of blanket. Block.

 = mc (Saffron)

■ = cc A (Sapphire)

■ = cc B (Serendipity Turquoise)

NOTE: Pattern in chart appears more elongated
than on completed blanket. This is because there
are more rows per inch than stitches per inch.

Start
here

Basketweave Blanket

Designed by Kathleen Case, Williamstown, MA

A tisket, a tasket, a basketweave blanket! Here's another classic pattern that's both cozy and reversible — the garter stitch border and the alternating knit and purl blocks look similar on both sides of the blanket. This is a great choice for a beginner who wants to create an interesting texture. The basketweave looks complex but is actually simple to knit.

Finished measurements: 30" (76cm) square

Yarn: Brown Sheep Cotton Fleece, 80% pima cotton / 20% merino wool, 750 yds (675m)

Needles: One #8 (5.0mm) circular needle, 24" (61cm) long, *or size needed to obtain gauge*

Gauge: 20 sts = 4" (10cm) in basketweave pattern

K = knit ◆ **P** = purl ◆ **st(s)** = stitch(es)

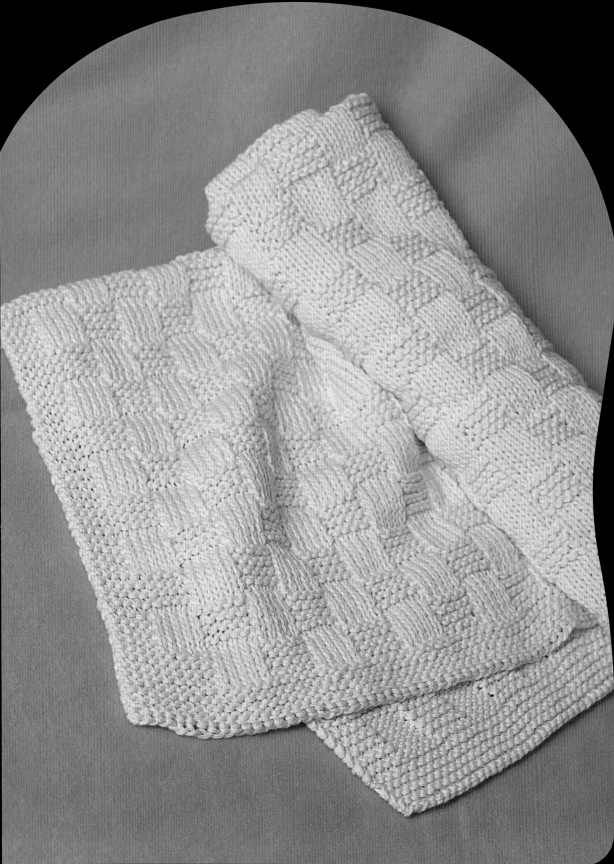

Cozy Cotton

The Brown Sheep Company yarn that was used to knit the blanket shown on page 53 is a blend consisting of 80 percent cotton and 20 percent merino wool. It knits up into a delightfully soft fabric that has a nice drape and is an excellent weight for a baby blanket. The yarn comes in a number of other pastels that are especially nice for baby items (shown on this page), or look for some of the jazzy, hot colors the yarn comes in as well. Blankets knit with this yarn must be hand-washed in cool water.

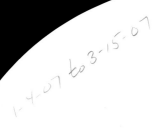

KNITTING THE BOTTOM BORDER

Cast on 150 sts.

Rows 1–10: Knit to the end of each row.

KNITTING THE BLANKET BODY

Row 1 and all odd-numbered rows: Knit to the end of each row.

Rows 2, 4, 6, and 8: K5, *K5, P5; repeat from * to last 5 sts; K5.

Rows 10, 12, 14, and 16: K5, *P5, K5; repeat from * to last 5 sts; K5.

Repeat Rows 1–16 until the blanket measures about 28" (71cm), ending with Row 8 or Row 16.

KNITTING THE TOP BORDER

Rows 1–10: Knit to the end of each row.

Cast off all sts loosely. Weave in any ends.

Basketweave Pattern

It's hard to believe that this interestingly textured, weave-look pattern boils down to just two stitches: garter and stockinette. An entire pattern block consists of 16 rows, organized in 8-row bands of alternating garter and stockinette stitches. The smaller blocks formed by the garter and stockinette stitches shift at the completion of each band in order to create the over-under effect. By increasing the size of these blocks, you could achieve a bolder look. You might also like to experiment by knitting with two or more colors.

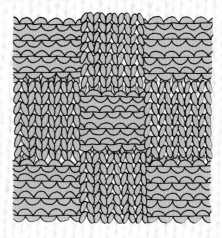

By the Pond

Designed by Barbara Telford, Woodsmoke Woolworks

This blanket is an entire lily pond, complete with cattails, bulrushes, grass, frogs, dragonflies, and lily pads. The center of the pond is knitted first, then the edges are picked up and the border is knitted in the round. Some of the vegetation is knitted into the border, but you can make any number of frogs, dragonflies, and lilies and arrange them in a way that suits your fancy. Just remember not to put the dragonflies too close to the frogs, so they won't be eaten!

Finished measurements: 35" (88cm) square

Yarn: Briggs & Little Regal, 100% wool, double-knit weight

    1211 yds (1090m) mc (medium blue)
    272 yds (249m) cc A (purple)
    272 yds (249m) cc B (medium green)
    272 yds (249m) cc C (dark green)
    272 yds (249m) cc D (brown)
    10 yds (9m) cc E (black)
    15 yds (14m) cc F (white, pink, red, or yellow)
    1 yd (1m) cc G (yellow)
    3 yds (3m) per dragonfly cc H (various light colors)
    2 yds (2m) per dragonfly cc I (various dark colors)

Needles

Five #7 (4.5mm) long circular needles, *or size needed to obtain gauge*

Set of five #7 (4.5mm) dp needles, *or same as above*

Set of two #4 (3.5mm) dp needles

One size G (4.0mm) crochet hook

Gauge: 20 sts = 4" (10cm) on #7 (4.5mm) needles in St st

Other supplies: Yarn needle; small amount of stuffing, such as polyester fill; Fray Check; 2 yds waste yarn (smaller size than main yarn and either cotton or synthetic); stitch markers

---

cc = contrasting color ◆ **dp** = double pointed ◆ **inc** = increase ◆ **K** = knit ◆ **K2tog** = knit 2 stitches together ◆ **mc** = main color ◆ **P** = purl ◆ **P2tog** = purl 2 stitches together ◆ **psso** = pass slip stitch over ◆ **sl** = slip ◆ **st(s)** = stitch(es) ◆ **St st** = stockinette stitch

KNITTING THE CENTER POND

With the #7 (4.5mm) circular needle and mc, cast on 104 sts.

Row 1: Knit.

Row 2: Purl.

Row 3: Knit.

Row 4: Change to waste yarn and knit.

Row 5: Using mc, knit to end of row.

Row 6: Purl.

Row 7: Sl 1, knit to last st, sl 1.

Row 8: Purl.

Repeat Rows 5–8 until you have 140 rows after the waste yarn row. Do not cast off.

KNITTING THE BORDER

Remove the waste yarn at the cast-on edge by pulling on one of its tails, and pick up the sts on one of the circular needles. To avoid losing stitches, remove the waste yarn a few stitches at a time, picking the live stitches up as you go. You should have 104 sts.

Using two more circular needles, pick up 104 sts along each side of the center pond. The slipped sts at the ends of the rows should make picking up sts easier.

You now have four needles, each with 104 sts, going around the pond. You will be knitting in the round with five circular needles, starting with the needle holding the 140th row of the center pond and knitting around as you would with straight dp needles. For color sequence, refer to Cattails Charts on pages 60–62. On each needle the first 4 stitches are from the right-corner chart, the next 96 stitches are 8 repeats of the center chart, and the last 4 stitches are from the left-corner chart, line 1 in each case.

The first st on each needle is the corner st. Note that the increases at the beginning of each row are made in the stitch following the corner stitch. Increase by knitting into the front and back of the stitch before taking it off the needle (see page 14).

NOTE: If you are using two-handed color changing, do not bring the yarn forward for the corner stitch or increase stitch. If this leaves too long a strand of yarn, keep the strand loose and pick it up on the next round. For further advice, see Colorful Effects on pages 19–21.

Round 1: Following Cattails Charts, on each needle K1, inc 1 in next st, knit to last st, inc 1. You will have 106 sts on each needle.

Round 2: K1, inc 1 in next st, knit to last st, inc 1. You will have 108 sts on each needle.

Round 3: K1, inc 1 in next st, knit to last st, inc 1. You will have 110 sts on each needle.

Round 4: Knit even to end of rnd.

Rounds 5–12: Repeat Rounds 1–4 two more times.

While working Cattails Charts and following instructions below, continue increasing at the beginning and end of each needle in Rounds 1–3 for the remainder of the border, until you have 176 sts on each needle.

MAKING THE CATTAILS

Round 13: Repeat Round 1.

Round 14: In addition to increasing at the ends of needles as established and changing colors for cattails, inc 1 in each cattail. Cattails now have 2 sts. (See Three-Dimensional Effects at right.)

Three-Dimensional Effects

To make the cattails look as if they're rising above the pond level, the number of stitches in each cattail is increased over several rounds, then reduced back to a single stitch. (These extra stitches do not appear on the charts.) Pull the blue yarn tightly behind the cattail, contrary to the usual rule for intarsia knitting, to help the cattails stand proud.

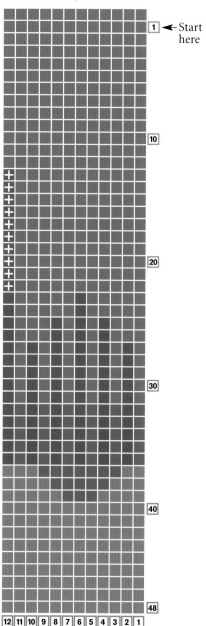

Round 15: In addition to increasing at the ends of needles as established, inc 1 in first st of each cattail. Cattails have 3 sts.

Round 16: Inc 1 in first 2 sts of each cattail. Cattails have 5 sts.

Rounds 17–19: Inc 1 at beginning and end of each needle, with no more increases in cattail sts.

Round 20: In each cattail, sl 1, K1, psso, K1, K2tog. Cattails have 3 sts.

Round 21: Repeat Round 1.

Round 22: In addition to increasing at the ends of needles as established, when you get to each cattail, sl 1, K2tog, psso. Each cattail has 1 st and you have 138 sts on each needle.

MAKING THE BULRUSHES

Rounds 23–36: Continue to follow Cattails Charts and to make increases at the beginnings and ends of needles every three out of four rows, as established. When the bulrushes reach the st next to the corner st, use cc B for the corner st as well.

At the end of the bulrush rounds, you will have 158 sts on each needle.

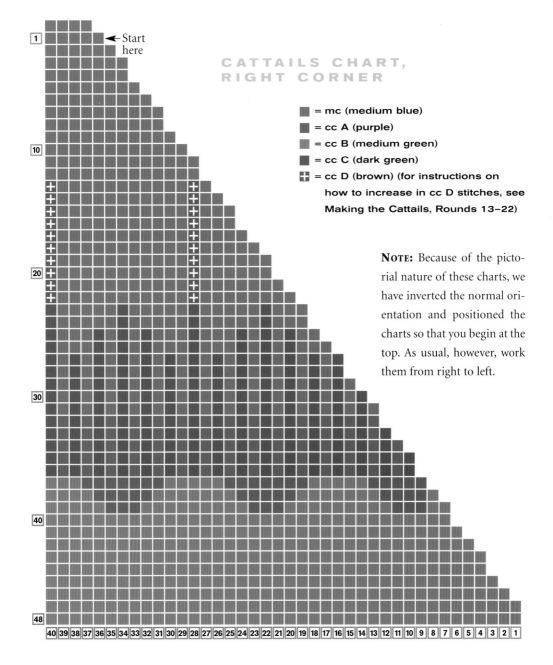

CATTAILS CHART,
RIGHT CORNER

■ = mc (medium blue)
■ = cc A (purple)
■ = cc B (medium green)
■ = cc C (dark green)
✚ = cc D (brown) (for instructions on
    how to increase in cc D stitches, see
    Making the Cattails, Rounds 13–22)

NOTE: Because of the pictorial nature of these charts, we have inverted the normal orientation and positioned the charts so that you begin at the top. As usual, however, work them from right to left.

Start here

CATTAILS CHART, LEFT CORNER

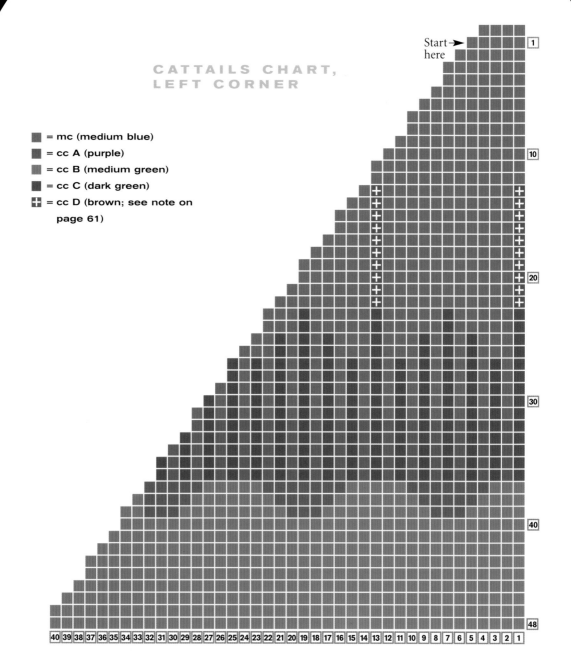

■ = mc (medium blue)
■ = cc A (purple)
■ = cc B (medium green)
■ = cc C (dark green)
✚ = cc D (brown; see note on page 61)

Rounds 37–42: Continue to make the established increases; follow the Cattails Chart to work the grasses. At the end of Round 42, you will have 168 sts on each needle.

Round 43: Inc 1, purl to last st, inc 1.

Round 44: Knit to end of rnd.

Round 45: Inc 1, purl to last st, inc 1.

Round 46: Inc 1, knit to last st, inc 1.

Round 47: Inc 1, purl to last st, inc 1. You will have 176 sts on each needle.

Round 48: Cast off knitwise.

MAKING THE FRONT HALF OF THE FROG

NOTE: Instructions are for one frog front. Make as many as you like. You can make half a frog to peek out from under a lily pad or keep on knitting to make a whole frog.

With the #4 (3.5mm) needles and cc B, cast on 5 sts.

Rows 1 and 3: Purl.

Row 2: In a knit row, inc 1 twice, inc 2 by knitting into the front, back, and front of the next stitch, inc 1 twice. You will have 11 sts.

Row 4: K4, make eye bobble, K1, make eye bobble, K4. (See Making Bobbles on page 68.)

Row 5: Inc 1 purlwise 5 times, P1, inc 1 purlwise 5 times. You will have 21 sts. (Purlwise increases are made by purling into the front and knitting into the back of the stitch.)

Row 6: K8, K2tog, K1, K2tog, K8. You will have 19 sts.

Rows 7, 9, and 11: Purl to end of each row.

Row 8: K7, K2tog, K1, K2tog, K7. You will have 17 sts.

Row 10: K6, K2tog, K1, K2tog, K6. You will have 15 sts.

To continue making the rest of the frog, skip to Making the Back Half of a Frog on page 64. If you are making the front half only, continue with Last Row, below.

Last Row: *Sl 1, K2tog, psso; repeat from * to the end of the row. You will have 5 sts.

To finish, cut the yarn and draw it through the remaining sts. Starting at the nose, sew the belly seam. Stuff the frog lightly and close the hole at the end.

To make the front legs, put the crochet hook through a stitch in Row 6, two rows back from the eye row and 4 sts in from the seam. Pick up an 8" (20cm) piece of yarn in the middle. Using both sides as a single piece of yarn, make 3 chains. On the next chain, pull only one strand of yarn through and tug as tightly as possible. Repeat on the other side of the frog. Use a fray-stopping product such as Fray Check on the ends of the arms.

MAKING THE BACK HALF OF THE FROG

Row 1: K5, K2tog, K1, K2tog, K5. You will have 13 sts.

Rows 2, 4, 6 and 8: Purl to the end of each row.

Row 3: K4, K2tog, K1, K2tog, K4. You will have 11 sts.

Row 5: K2, inc 2, K1, K2tog. Turn and work on these 7 sts to make the right leg. Keep the remaining 5 sts on the needle.

Rows 7 and 9: Knit.

Row 10: P2tog, sl 1, P2tog, psso, P2tog. You will have 3 sts.

Rows 11, 13, and 15: Knit.

Rows 12 and 14: Purl.

Row 16: Sl 1, P2tog, psso. You will have 1 st.

Row 17: Inc 2 knitwise to make 3 sts.

Rows 18 and 20: Purl.

Row 19: K1, inc 2, K1. You will have 5 sts.

After Row 20, cast off knitwise.

To make the left leg, work on the 5 sts remaining from Row 4.

Row 5 (second leg): K2, inc 2, K2. Turn and work on these 7 sts to make the left leg.

Rows 6–20 (second leg): Work the same as the right leg and cast off knitwise.

To finish, cut the yarn and draw it through the remaining sts. Starting at the nose, sew the belly seam to the beginning of the legs. Stuff the frog lightly and close the hole at the end. Crochet the front legs as described above.

MAKING A DRAGONFLY

NOTE: Instructions are for one dragonfly. Make as many as you like. I like to use up snippets of yarn and make them in different colors. Generally, the bodies (cc H) should be light colored, and the wings (cc I) dark colored.

With the #4 (3.5mm) needles and cc H, cast on 4 sts and make a 2" (5cm) I-cord. (See Making an I-Cord, facing page.)

When the I-cord reaches the right length, turn the work and begin flat knitting.

Row 1: Inc 1 in each of the first 3 sts purlwise, P1. You will have 7 sts.

Row 2: K2, inc 1, K1, inc 1, K2. You will have 9 sts.

Row 3: Purl.

Row 4: K3, make wing bobble, K1, make wing bobble, K3. (See Making Bobbles on page 68.) Use cc J for wings.

Row 5: Purl.

Row 6: K3, make wing bobble, K1, make wing bobble, K3. Use cc J for wings.

Row 7: P2tog twice, P1, P2tog twice. You will have 5 sts.

Row 8: K1, make eye bobble, K1, make eye bobble, K1. (See Making Bobbles, page 68.) Use cc E for eyes.

Row 9: P2tog, P1, P2tog. You will have 3 sts.

Cut the yarn and draw it through the remaining 3 sts. Starting at the nose, sew the belly seam. Stuff the fly lightly and close the hole.

MAKING A LILY PAD

NOTE: Lily pads come in three different sizes. Make as many as you like, in a variety of sizes. Flowers look best on the large lily pads. The pads are knit in the round from the center of five dp needles.

With the #7 (4.5mm) dp needles and cc C, cast on 4 sts.

Row 1: Inc 1 in each st purlwise. You will have 8 sts.

Row 2: Inc 1 in each st knitwise. You will have 16 sts.

Row 3: Purl.

Distribute the sts evenly among four needles and begin knitting in the round.

Round 1: On each needle, (K1, inc 1) twice. You will have 6 sts on each needle.

Rounds 2, 4, 7, and 9: Knit.

Round 3: (K2, inc 1) twice. You will have 8 sts on each needle.

Round 5: K1, inc 1, K3, inc 1, K2. You will have 10 sts on each needle.

Round 6: (K4, inc 1) twice. You will have 12 sts on each needle.

Round 8: (K3, inc 1) 3 times. You will have 15 sts on each needle.

For small lily pad, cast off knitwise.

Round 10: K2, inc 1, (K4, inc 1) twice, K2. You will have 18 sts on each needle.

Rounds 11 and 13: Knit.

Making an I-Cord

I-cords are narrow tubes knitted on two double-pointed needles. The project directions will specify the number of stitches – usually 3 or 4.

1. Using double-pointed needles, cast on the number of stitches indicated in the pattern and knit those stitches.
2. *Do not turn the needle.* Instead, place the needle with the stitches in your left hand and slide the stitches to the right to the tip of the needle, so that the yarn comes from the last stitch at the left. Insert the right needle, knitwise, into the first stitch, pull the yarn firmly across the back, and knit the stitch in the usual manner. Make sure you knit this stitch snugly. (See drawing below.)
3. Knit the remaining stitches on the needle.
4. Repeat steps 2 and 3 until the I-cord is the desired length.

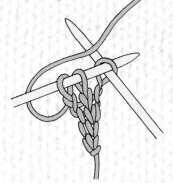

Making Bobbles

The frogs' eyes, the dragonflies' eyes and wings, and the centers of the flowers are bobbles knitted into the patterns. Bobbles are made by knitting several stitches into a single stitch, working on only those expanded stitches for one or more rows, then reducing them back into a single stitch.

To make the eye bobble, use cc E to knit 4 sts into the marked st (knit into the front, back, front, and back again before slipping all the stitches from the needle.). Turn and P4, then turn again and K4 with cc B, turn and P4, turn and K4tog through the back. Still using cc B, pick up and knit the st you originally knitted into, then pass the bobble st over it.

To make the dragonfly's first wing bobble, use cc I to knit 2 sts into the marked st.

Work on these 2 sts in St st for 19 rows, starting and ending with purl rows, then K2tog through the back. Using cc H, pick up and knit the st you originally knitted into, then pass the bobble st over it.

To make the dragonfly's second wing bobble, use cc I to knit 2 sts into the st. Work on these 2 sts in St st for 19 rows, starting and ending with purl rows. On the next row, with cc H pick up and knit the st you originally knitted into, knit the 2 wing sts together, then pass the previous st over it.

To make the flower bobble, use cc G to knit 4 sts into the picked-up st (knit into the front, back, front, and back again). Turn and P4, then turn again and K4 with cc B, turn and P4, turn and K4tog through the back.

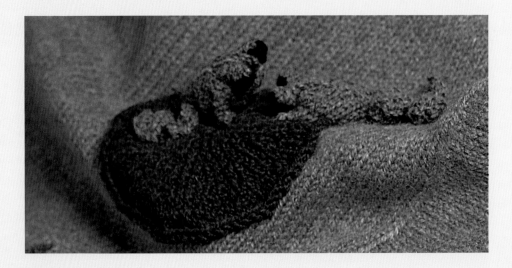

Round 12: K4, inc 1, (K5, inc 1) twice, K1. You will have 21 sts on each needle.

For medium lily pad, cast off knitwise.

Round 14: K2, inc 1, (K6, inc 1) twice, K4. You will have 24 sts on each needle.

Round 15: Knit.

Round 16: K3, inc 1, (K5, inc 1) 3 times, K2. You will have 28 sts on each needle.

For large lily pad, cast off knitwise.

MAKING A WATER LILY

With the #7 (4.5mm) dp needles and cc F, cast on 45 sts.

Change to the #4 (3.5mm) needles.

Row 1, petal 1: P5, turn, K1, turn, P2, turn, K3, turn, P4, turn, K5, turn, P6, turn, K7, turn, P8, turn, K9, turn, P2, P2tog, P1, P2tog, P2.

Continue until you have five petals and you have used up all the sts on the larger needle. You should have 35 sts on the smaller needle.

Row 2: *K2tog, sl 1, K2tog, psso, K2tog; repeat from * to end of row. You will have 15 sts.

Row 3: *Sl 1, K2tog, psso; repeat from * to end of row. You will have 5 sts.

Cut the yarn and draw it through the remaining 5 sts. Pull tightly and sew the ends together.

To make the center of the flower, with the #7 (4.5mm) needles and cc G, pick up and knit 1 st in the middle of the flower (with the knit side up). Make a bobble in this stitch (see Making Bobbles on page 68).

Cut the yarn and pull it through the remaining st. With a yarn needle, pull the loose ends through to the wrong side of the flower, then through the center of the lily pad. Weave in the loose ends.

FINISHING UP

Sew water lilies, frogs, and dragonflies to the large lily pads, then attach the lily pads to the blanket using a running stitch just inside the lily pad cast-off round. Loose ends can be buried beneath the lily pads.

Jelly Beans

Designed by Dori Betjemann, Florence, MA

In this blanket, four bright colors are worked together in a slipped moss stitch that looks like tiny jelly beans. Although the colors appear to be intertwined, you actually work with only one color at a time — you don't have to worry about carrying several colors or winding multiple bobbins. The central panel is knitted first, with nine "jelly bean" sections alternating with solid-colored bands. The border of triangular pennants is knitted separately, and then joined to the central panel using double-pointed needles.

Finished measurements: 28" by 32" (71cm by 81cm)

Yarn: Plymouth Cleckheaton Country 8 ply, 100% machine-washable wool

630 yds (567m) mc (turquoise/#2230)

420 yds (378m) cc A (periwinkle/#1860)

420 yds (378m) cc B (natural/#0050)

420 yds (378m) cc C (pink/#1977)

Needles

One # 9 (5.5mm) circular needle, 32" (81cm) long, *or size needle to obtain gauge*

Two #6 (4.0mm) circular needles, 32" (81cm) long

One set #6 (4.0mm) dp needles

Gauge: 26 sts = 4" (10cm) on #9 (5.5mm) needles in jelly bean stitch

Other supplies: Yarn needle

---

cc = contrasting color ◆ **dp** = double pointed ◆ **inc** = increase ◆ **K** = knit **mc** = main color ◆ **P** = purl ◆ **sl** = slip **st(s)** = stitch(es) ◆ **St st** = stockinette stitch ◆ **yb** = yarn back ◆ **yf** = yarn forward

MAKING THE BOTTOM EDGE OF THE PANEL

With the #9 (5.5mm) needle and mc, cast on 157 sts and purl 1 row (wrong side).

MAKING THE JELLY BEANS

NOTE: Be sure you always hold the working yarn on the wrong side of the piece when you slip stitches in the pattern area. Slip stitches purlwise.

Row 1 (right side): With mc, K1, *yb, sl 1, K1; repeat from * to end of row.

Row 2: With mc, K1, *yf, sl 1, K1; repeat from * to end of row.

Row 3: With cc A, K2, *yb, sl 1, K1; repeat from * to the last st; K1.

Row 4: With cc A, K2, *yf, sl 1, K1; repeat from * to the last st; K1.

Rows 5 and 6: Repeat Rows 1 and 2 with cc B.

Rows 7 and 8: Repeat Rows 3 and 4 with cc C.

Rows 9–32: Repeat Rows 1–8 three more times.

Rows 33 and 34: Repeat Rows 1 and 2.

MAKING THE SOLID STRIPE

Change to the #6 (4.0mm) needle and mc.

Rows 1 and 2: Knit to the end of each row.

Rows 3 and 4: Purl to the end of each row.

FINISHING THE PANEL

Work 8 more jelly bean sections and 7 more solid stripes.

After the final jelly bean section, with #6 (4.0mm) needle and mc, knit 1 row. Cast off all sts.

MAKING THE BOTTOM BORDER

NOTE: All increase sts in this section are made by knitting into the front and back of the same st (see page 14). Work back and forth on a circular needle.

With one of the #6 (4.0mm) circular needles and mc, cast on 2 sts.

Row 1 (wrong side): K2.

Row 2: Inc 1, K1. You will have 3 sts.

Row 3: Inc 1, K2. You will have 4 sts.

Row 4: Inc 1, K3. You will have 5 sts.

Continue, increasing in the first st of each row, until you have 12 sts: one pennant.

Cut the yarn and turn the needle, leaving the pendant stitches on the left-hand needle. Again cast on 2 sts. Repeat from Row 1 to make the next pennant.

When you have 13 pennants (156 sts), knit straight across them for 5 rows. Weave in the ends on the wrong side as you come to them. Leave the sts on the needle.

With mc and the #6 (4.0mm) dp needles, cast on 3 sts.

Row 1: K2, sl 1 knitwise. Set aside.

Using the other #6 (4.0mm) circular needle and with the right side facing you, pick up 156 sts from the bottom (cast-on) edge of the panel.

Place the straight edge of the border against the bottom edge of the panel, wrong sides together and needles parallel.

Insert the dp needle with the 3 sts on it through 1 st on the panel and 1 st on the border, and knit them together with mc.

Pass the sl st over the knit st. You now have 3 sts on the dp needle.

Slide the 3 sts back to the beginning of the dp needle without turning the needle.

Repeat until all the panel and border sts have been knitted and cast off, then cast off the remaining 3 sts.

MAKING AND JOINING THE TOP BORDER

Knit the top border following the same method as the bottom border and join it to the top (cast-off) edge of the center panel.

MAKING AND JOINING THE SIDE BORDERS

Knit the side borders following the same method as the top and bottom borders, but make 14 pennants (168 sts) for each side.

To join the side borders, pick up 168 sts from the sides of the panel and knit them to the borders as you did with the top and bottom borders.

FINISHING

Sew the loose edges together neatly at the corners of the blanket, and weave in all the ends.

Handling Four Colors

You may carry the colors up the side instead of cutting them when not in use. Be sure to bring the new active yarn from *beneath* the other colors. If you choose to cut the old color yarns, instead, leave a tail of 6 to 8" (15 to 20cm). Knit the first stitch with the new color, leaving another tail of the same length. Hold the two tails tightly between the third and fourth fingers of your right hand.

On the next knit stitch, maintain tension on the two tails and twist them around the working yarn just before you knit the stitch. Do this for 5 or 6 sts.

Striped Receiving Blanket

Designed by Linda Daniels, Northampton Wools

If you ever doubted that the simplest of techniques can yield beautiful results, this blanket proves the case once and for all. There's nothing to it except straight stockinette knitting, but the blanket is memorable because of the way the three colors shift in each section of paired stripes. If you're feeling adventurous, try using more colors or varying the width of the stripes. The versions shown opposite and on page 76 are in double-knit yarn, but fingering wool will give you a softer, lighter-weight blanket.

Finished measurement: 30" by 30" (76cm by 76cm)

Fingering-Weight Yarn

485 yds (437m) mc; 345 yds (310m) cc A; 345 yds (310m) cc B

Needles for fingering-yarn version

One #3 (3.25mm) circular needle 24" (61 cm) long, *or size needed to obtain gauge*

Gauge for fingering-yarn version: 28 sts = 4" (10cm) in St st

Worsted-Weight Yarn (pictured on pages 75 and 76)

Brown Sheep Lamb's Pride Superwash, 100% wool

410 yds (369m) mc (p. 75, Plum Crazy; p. 76, Alabaster)

290 yds (261m) cc A (p. 75, Lemon Ice; p. 76, Misty Blue)

290 yds (261m) cc B (p 75, Rose Quartz; p. 76, Lemon Ice)

Needles for worsted-yarn version

One #7 (4.25mm) circular needle, 24" (61 cm) long, *or size needed to obtain gauge*

Gauge for worsted-yarn version: 20 sts = 4" (10cm) in St st

Other supplies: Size 4(E) or 6(G) crochet hook

---

cc = contrasting color ◆ **mc** = main color
st = stitch ◆ **St st** = stockinette stitch

WORKING THE CENTER PANEL	FINGERING	WORSTED
With cc A, cast on	190 sts	136 sts
Work the striped panel in stockinette stitch throughout (knit 1 row, purl 1 row), following the Stripes Chart on page 79 for color changes. Begin chart at bottom right. Work each color for	4 rows	2 rows
Work color blocks A–F	once	once
Complete the panel by working color blocks	A–C	A–F
Piece will measure about	31" (79cm)	29" (74cm)

Garter Stitch Border (shown on page 75)

WORKING THE TOP BORDER	FINGERING	WORSTED
Rows 1, 3, 5, and 7 (right side): With mc, and using stitches on needle at top of panel, inc 1 by knitting into the front and back of first stitch on needle, knit to last stitch, inc 1.		
Rows 2, 4, 6, and 8: Knit to end of row. After Row 8 is completed, you will have 4 garter stitch ridges on the right side, and on the needle you will have	198 sts	144 sts
Picot Fringe: Cast off as follows: K2, bind off 1 by slipping first stitch over second; *slip remaining stitch back onto left-hand needle, cast on 3 sts by inserting the needle between the first and second stitches and knitting a new stitch, bind off 5 sts; repeat from * until 1 stitch remains. Draw the yarn end through this stitch to fasten off.		
WORKING THE BOTTOM BORDER		
Row 1: Using mc, and with right side facing you, pick up and knit along the bottom (cast-on) edge	192 sts	138 sts

	FINGERING	WORSTED
Rows 2–8: Repeat Rows 2–8 under Working the Top Border, above. You will have	198 sts	144 sts
Cast off as for top border.		
WORKING THE SIDE BORDERS		
Row 1: Using mc, and with right side facing you, pick up and knit along each edge	218 sts	146 sts
Rows 2–8: Repeat Rows 2–8 under Working the Top Border, above. You will have	226 sts	154 sts
Cast off as for top border.		
FINISHING		
Sew corner edges together with an invisible stitch. Weave in all loose ends.		

Picot Edge Border *(shown on page 76)*

WORKING THE TOP BORDER	FINGERING	WORSTED
Row 1 (right side): With mc, using stitches on needle at top of panel, inc 1 in first stitch by knitting into the front and back of it, knit to last stitch, inc 1.		
Rows 2 and 4: Purl.		
Rows 3 and 5: Repeat Row 1. You will have	196 sts	142 sts
Row 6: Change to cc A and purl to end of row.		
Row 7 (right side): K1, *YO, K2tog; repeat from * to last stitch; K1.		

Stripe Hype

Designing with stripes is an easy way to get interesting color combinations into knitted projects without the fuss of carrying yarns or winding bobbins. In this project, there's no need to cut the yarn each time you change color within each of the color blocks – just carry it up the edge by wrapping the two colors once around each other before starting across the row with the new color.

For instance, with the worsted-weight yarn, you'll knit 2 rows of yellow, then join purple. Wrap the yellow and purple yarn before knitting across the row with purple. When you come back and are ready to begin the next yellow row, wrap the two yarns again, leaving the purple behind. When you reach the next color block that does not use one of those colors, cut the old yarn and weave it into the back of the piece.

NOTE: Knit each stripe in the Stripes Chart at the right for four rows in fingering-weight yarn and for two rows in worsted-weight yarn.

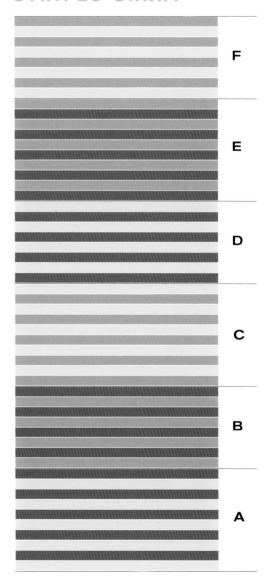

F

E

D

C

B

A

	FINGERING	WORSTED
Rows 8 and 10: Purl to end of row.		
Row 9: Knit to end of row.		
Row 11: Change to mc. K2tog, knit to last 2 sts, ssk.		
Rows 12 and 14: Purl to end of row.		
Rows 13 and 15: Repeat Row 11. You will have	190 sts	136 sts
Cast off.		
WORKING THE BOTTOM BORDER		
Row 1: Using mc and working from the right side along the bottom (cast-on) edge, pick up	192 sts	138 sts
Rows 2–15: Repeat Rows 2–15 under Working the Top Border, above.		
Cast off.		
WORKING THE SIDE BORDERS		
Row 1: Using mc and working from the right side along each edge, pick up	218 sts	146 sts
Rows 2–15: Repeat Rows 2–15 under Working the Top Border, above.		
After Row 5, you will have	222 sts	150 sts
After Row 15, you will have	216 sts	144 sts
Cast off.		
FINISHING		
Turn back the border by folding it, wrong sides together, along the picot edge. Use mc to stitch the border in place with an overcast stitch. Sew corner edges together on both the front and back of the blanket with an invisible stitch. Weave in all loose ends.		

Sheep Dreams

Designed by Dori Betjemann, Florence, MA

Fluffy sheep graze peacefully in their pens all around the edges of this blanket. The design could serve as a knitting sampler, featuring three fancy stitches in addition to stockinette stitch — a ribbed stitch for the border, a double-bind stitch for the walls of the sheep's pens, and a checkered stitch for the central panel (see page 84). The sheep are added in duplicate stitch after the blanket is completed.

Finished measurements: 26" by 32" (66cm by 81cm)

Yarn: Brown Sheep Lamb's Pride Superwash, 100% wool, worsted weight

800 yds (720m) mc (Shane's Red)

15 yds (14m) cc A (Onyx)

Brown Sheep Berrocco Plush

90 yds (81m) cc B (Natural)

Needles: One #7 (4.5mm) circular needle, 32" (61cm) or 40" (101.5mm) long, *or size needed to obtain gauge*

Gauge: 18 sts = 4" (10cm) on #7 (4.5mm) needles in St st

Other supplies: Yarn needle, stitch markers, 8–12 bobbins if intarsia is used

---

f&b = front and back ◆ **DB** = double bind (see page 84) ◆ **K** = knit ◆ **K2tog** = knit 2 stitches together ◆ **P** = purl ◆ **P2tog** = purl 2 stitches together ◆ **sl** = slip ◆ **st(s)** = stitch(es) ◆ **St st** = stockinette stitch

A Sampler in Action

Ribbed Stitch
(multiple of 2 sts +1)

Row 1 (right side): Inc 1 knitwise by knitting into the front and back of every st.
Row 2: K2tog; *P2tog, K2tog; repeat from *.
Repeat these 2 rows.

Ribbed stitch

Double Bind

YO, K2, pass YO stitch over the 2 knitted stitches.

Double bind

Checkered Stitch
(multiple of 3 sts +1)

Row 1 (right side): Knit.
Rows 2 and 4: Purl.
Row 3: K1; *P2, K1; repeat from *.
Repeat these 4 rows.

Checkered stitch

KNITTING THE BOTTOM BORDER

NOTE: After Row 10, the first and last 10 sts of each row (not counting expanded sts) are the side borders and will be repeated until you reach the top border. We refer to them throughout as "border."

With mc and the #7 (4.5mm) circular needle, cast on 119 sts.

Rows 1–9: Work in ribbed stitch (see A Sampler in Action, page 84) to the end of each row.

Row 10: Work in ribbed stitch to the last 2 sts, K2.

Row 11: Work in ribbed stitch for 7 sts, place marker, K1, inc 1 by knitting into the front and back of the next stitch, place marker, knit to last 10 sts, place marker, K3, place marker, work in ribbed stitch for 7 sts. You will have 120 sts.

Rows 12 and 14: Work in ribbed stitch to marker, move marker, P3, move marker, purl to next marker, move marker, P3, move marker, work in ribbed stitch to end.

Row 13: Work in ribbed stitch for 7 sts, move marker, K3, move marker, knit to last 10 sts, move marker, K3, move marker, work in ribbed stitch to end.

KNITTING THE BOTTOM SQUARES

NOTE: You may find it helpful to use additional markers to separate the chart repeats in this section (that is, after stitch 38, then after every 24 sts across to the border sts).

NOTE: The sheep motifs are added in duplicate stitch after the blanket is finished. (For Duplicate Stitching, see page 88.)

If you prefer, you can work the sheep into the design using the intarsia method while you knit the blanket (see Colorful Effects, pages 19–21). If you choose this approach, be sure to bring the new color up from underneath the strand of color being dropped when a new color is needed (see illustration on page 20). If the two strands are not twisted, a hole forms at the juncture of the two colors.

Rows 1 and 3: Work 10 border sts as established, then work double bind (DB; see A Sampler in Action, page 84) to last 10 sts, work border.

Rows 2 and all even-numbered rows through Row 34: Work border, purl to last 10 sts, work border.

Row 5 and all odd-numbered rows through Row 31: Work border, DB2, *K20, DB2; repeat from * to last 10 sts; work border.

Rows 33 and 35: Repeat Rows 1 and 3.

NOTE: Since the top of one square is also the bottom of the square above it, we identify the first row of each new square as Row 4 for convenience in following the charts on pages 90–91.

Row 4 and all even-numbered rows to Row 34: Work border, purl to last 10 sts, work border. Reposition center markers to assist new layout (that is, after stitch 38 and before the last 38 sts).

Row 5 and all odd-numbered rows through Row 31: Work border, DB2, K20, DB2, K5, work in checkered stitch (see A Sampler in Action, page 84) for 34 sts, K5, DB2, K20, DB2, work border.

Rows 33 and 35: Work border, work double bind to last 10 sts, work border.

Next rows: Repeat Rows 4–35 two more times. You will have four squares along the bottom and three squares along the sides.

TOP SQUARES

Row 4 and all even-numbered rows: Work border, purl to last 10 sts, work border. Reposition markers again as for blocks across the bottom.

Row 5 and all odd-numbered rows through Row 31: Work border, DB2, *K20, DB2; repeat from * to last 10 sts; border.

Rows 33 and 35: Work border, DB to last 10 sts, work border.

KNITTING THE TOP BORDER

Rows 1 and 3: Work border, knit to last 10 sts, work border.

Row 2: Work border, purl to last 10 sts, work border.

Row 4: Work border, purl to last 7 sts, K2tog, P2tog, K3tog. You will have 119 sts.

Rows 5–14: Work in ribbed stitch to the end of each row.

FINISHING

Cast off loosely, cut the yarn, and weave in all the ends.

If you are working the sheep in duplicate stitch, do so now. (See page 88 for guidance and follow the Sheep Charts on pages 90–91.) Note that all the sheep face in toward the center of the blanket.

Duplicate Stitching

To work duplicate stitch, bring the threaded tapestry needle out from the center of the stitch below the stitch to be covered (see Step 1, below). Insert the needle through both sides of the "V" of the stitch above the one to be covered and pull the yarn through, thus covering half the stitch (see Step 2). Insert the needle again into the original hole (that is, the center of the stitch below the stitch being covered). Work from the bottom to the top to cover vertical stitches and from right to left and then left to right to cover horizontal stitches.

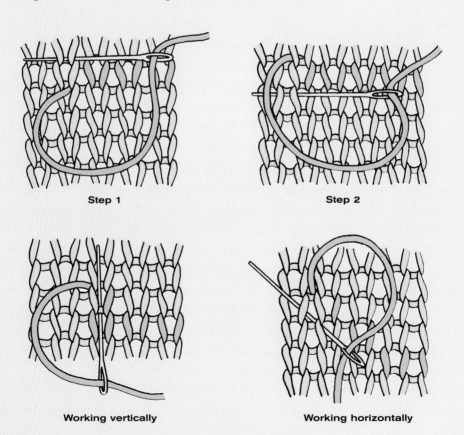

Step 1

Step 2

Working vertically

Working horizontally

Border			
Left Chart 1	Left Chart 1	Right Chart 2	Right Chart 2
Left Chart 1	Center Checkered Stitch Pattern		Right Chart 2
Left Chart 1			Right Chart 2
Left Chart 1			Right Chart 2
Left Chart 1	Left Chart 1	Right Chart 2	Right Chart 2

SHEEP CHART 1

(left side of blanket)

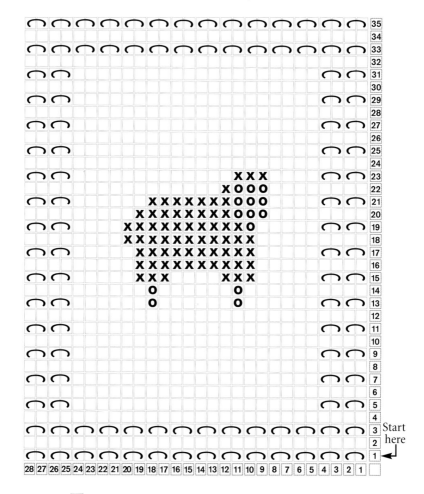

- ☐ = K on right side, P on wrong side mc
- ⌒ = DB (YO, K2, pass the YO the 2 knit sts)
- **O** = cc A
- **X** = cc B

SHEEP CHART 2

(right side of blanket)

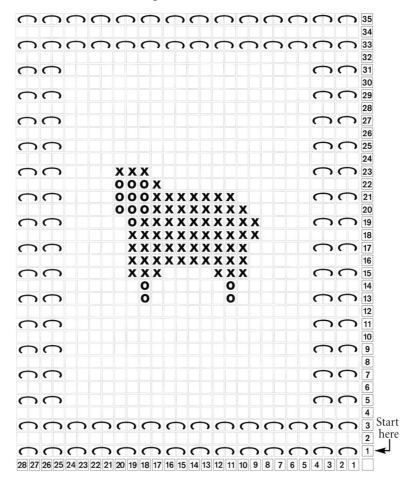

Baby Poncho

Designed by Beverly Galeskas, Fiber Trends

This elegant poncho is knit from the center out. You start with the front panel, hood, and back panel, then add the stripe, the sleeves, and finally the border. Optional buttons keep the sleeves closed and the poncho in place, and the hood can be pulled up in bad weather. Contrasting stitch patterns and colors make this poncho not only eye-catching, but also a fun and interesting project to knit.

Finished measurements: 15" by 25" (38cm by 63.5cm). Fits 6 months to 3 or 4 years old.

Yarn: Brown Sheep Lamb's Pride Superwash, 100% wool, worsted weight

435 yds (390m) mc (Alabaster)

350 yds (315m) cc A (Sunflower)

110 yds (81m) cc B (Lemon Ice)

Needles

One #7 (4.5mm) circular needle, 29" (73.5cm) or longer, *or size needed to obtain gauge*

Straight #7 (4.5mm) needles may be used for all parts of the poncho except the border

One extra #7 (4.5mm) straight needle

Gauge: 18 sts = 4" (10cm) on #7 (4.5mm) needles in front panel pattern stitch

Other supplies: 4 buttons, pins or cc threads for markers, stitch holder

---

cc = contrasting color ◆ **inc** = increase ◆ **K** = knit ◆ **K2tog** = knit 2 stitches together
P = purl ◆ **M1** = make 1 stitch ◆ **mc** = main color ◆ **ssk** = slip, slip, knit the 2 slipped stitches together ◆ **st(s)** = stitch(es)

MAKING THE FRONT PANEL

With mc and straight or circular #7 (4.5mm) needles, cast on 24 sts.

Row 1: K1, *P2, K2; repeat from * to last 3 sts; P2, K1.

Row 2: P1, *K2, P2; repeat from * to last 3 sts; K2, P1.

Row 3: Knit to end of row.

Row 4: Purl to end of row.

Row 5: K3, *P2, K2; repeat from * to last 5 sts; P2, K3.

Row 6: P3, *K2, P2; repeat from * to last 5 sts; K2, P3.

Rows 7 and 8: Repeat Rows 3 and 4.

Repeat these 8 rows until you have 66 rows, ending after a Row 2.

MAKING THE HOOD

Cut the mc yarn. With right side facing, join cc A, then knit even for 40 rows. You should have 20 garter st ridges.

At the beginning of a right-side row, cast on 12 sts. You will have 36 sts.

Knit even for 2 rows (1 garter st ridge).

Next row (right side): (K1, inc 1 in next 3 sts) 4 times, then knit to end of row.

Continue working in garter st for an additional 129 rows. You should have 66 garter st ridges from where you cast on. Mark the 34th ridge as the center top of the hood.

Next row (right side): (K1, K2tog, K2tog, K2tog) 4 times, then knit to end of row.

Next row: Knit.

Next row: Cast off 12 sts, knit to end of row. You will have 24 sts.

Work even in garter st for 38 more rows (19 more ridges), then cast off on next row.

Cut the yarn, leaving an 18" (45cm) tail for sewing the seam. Place the left collar under the right collar with both halves right-side up, match the corners, and pin the two ends together. (See diagram, Sewing the Hood, on facing page.)

Sew the cast-off edge to the first row of the right collar.

To make the center back seam, fold the hood in half along the ridge you marked and sew a flat seam, matching the garter st ridges. (See diagram, Sewing the Hood, on facing page.)

MAKING THE BACK PANEL

With mc, and right side facing you, pick up and knit 24 sts across the back neck edge of the hood. Purl 1 row.

Work in the same pattern that you used for the front panel for 98 rows, starting with pattern Row 1 and ending after pattern Row 2. Cast off and cut the yarn.

KNITTING THE LEFT SIDE

Row 1: The sides of the poncho are knitted perpendicular to the panels and hood. Beginning at the bottom left of the front panel with the right side facing you, pick up and knit in cc B: 40 sts along the front panel, 1 st at the corner of the collar (be sure to knit through both layers), 20 sts along the side of the top layer of the collar, 1 st at the corner of the hood and back panel, and 61 sts along the side of the back panel, ending at the lower edge. You will have 123 sts.

Rows 2, 3, and 4: Knit to end of each row. You will have 2 garter st ridges.

Row 5 (wrong side): P4, K1, *P5, K1; repeat from * to last 4 sts; P4. (Refer to Side Stitch Pattern, page 97, for a graphic representation of Rows 5–10.)

Row 6: K3, P1, *K1, P1, K3, P1; repeat from * to last 5 sts; K1, P1, K3.

Rows 7 and 8: K1, *P1, K1; repeat from * to end of each row.

Row 9: K1, P1, K1, P2, *P1, K1, P1, K1, P2; repeat from * to last 4 sts; P1, K1, P1, K1.

Row 10: K1, P1, K2, *K3, P1, K2; repeat from * to last 5 sts; K3, P1, K1.

Sewing the Hood

Lay the hood out on a flat surface to make sure the shawl collar is folded properly. Have the front panel right-side out and place the left collar under it, also right-side up. Match corners X to X and Y to Y. Pin in place, then turn over and sew cast-off edge of left collar to first row of right collar.

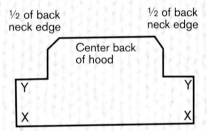

½ of back neck edge   ½ of back neck edge

Center back of hood

Y   Y

X   X

Face edge of hood

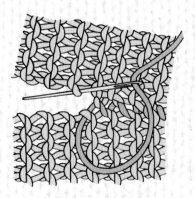

Sewing to make the center back seam

Rows 11, 12, 13, and 14: Purl to end of each row. You will have 2 garter st ridges.

Cut the yarn and slide sts to the other needle (or other end of the needle, if you are using a circular needle) so that the next row begins on the right side.

Row 15: Using mc, knit to end of row.

Row 16 and all other even-numbered rows through Row 32: Purl to end of each row.

Row 17: K1, ssk, *P5, K3; repeat from * to last 8 sts; P5, K2tog, K1. You now have 121 sts and will continue to decrease 2 sts in each odd-numbered row.

Rows 19, 23, 27, and 31: K1, ssk, knit to last 3 sts, K2tog, K1.

Row 21: K1, ssk, K2, *P5, K3; repeat from * to last 10 sts; P5, K2, K2tog, K1.

Row 25: K1, ssk, P1, *K3, P5; repeat from * to last 7 sts; K3, P1, K2tog, K1.

Row 29: K1, ssk, P3, *K3, P5; repeat from * to last 9 sts; K3, P3, K2tog, K1.

At the end of Row 32, you will have 107 sts.

Rows 33–48: Repeat Rows 17–32. You will have 91 sts.

Rows 49–62: Repeat rows 17–30. You will have 77 sts.

Row 67: *K2, K2tog; repeat from * to last 5 sts; K2, K2tog, K1. You will have 58 sts.

Mark the first and last sts with pins or cc thread, then cut yarn and slide sts onto a spare needle.

KNITTING THE RIGHT SIDE

Beginning at the bottom right of the back panel with the right side facing you, pick up and knit with cc B: 61 sts along the back panel, 1 st at the corner of the hood and back panel, 20 sts along the side of the lower layer of the collar, 1 st at the corner of the collar (be sure to knit through both layers), and 40 sts along the side of the front panel, ending at the lower edge. You will have 123 sts.

Work the right side to match the left side.

KNITTING THE BORDERS

Join cc A at the bottom right of the back panel with the right side facing you. Pick up and knit 324 sts onto the circular needle. Follow the diagram at right for distribution of stitches and placement of markers. (Work the left side sts off the spare needle.)

Rows 1, 3, 5, and 7 (wrong side): With cc A, knit to end of each row.

Rows 2, 4, 6, and 8: *Knit to first marked st, M1, K1, M1; repeat from * for each marked corner st; knit to end.

Cast off loosely knitwise.

FINISHING UP

Sew the short ends of the border band together and weave in all the yarn ends.

To hold the poncho straight when it is worn, sew buttons about 4" (10cm) down from the top fold to create sleeves. Use two buttons on each side, one on front and one on back, and sew them together through both layers.

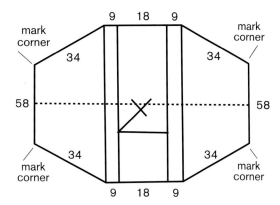

Side Stitch Pattern

Odd numbers are wrong-side rows; read chart from left to right.

Even numbers are right-side rows; read chart from right to left.

☐ = Purl on right side, knit on wrong side.

☐ = Knit on right side, purl on wrong side.

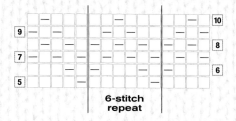

6-stitch repeat

COLOR AND PATTERN PLACEMENT

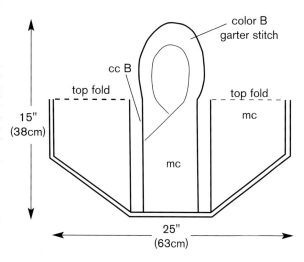

97

Felted Carriage Blanket

Designed by Gwen Steege, Williamstown, MA

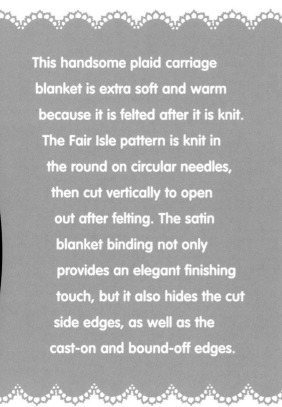

This handsome plaid carriage blanket is extra soft and warm because it is felted after it is knit. The Fair Isle pattern is knit in the round on circular needles, then cut vertically to open out after felting. The satin blanket binding not only provides an elegant finishing touch, but it also hides the cut side edges, as well as the cast-on and bound-off edges.

Size before felting: 32" by 33" (81cm by 84cm)

Finished size, after felting: 29" by 30" (74cm by 76cm)

Yarn: Brown Sheep's Lamb's Pride, 85% wool, 15% mohair, worsted weight

760 yds (684m) mc (Victorian Pink)

570 yds (513m) cc A (Sun Yellow)

570 yds (513m) cc B (Winter Blue)

190 yds (171m) cc C (Spruce)

190 yds (171m) cc D (Aran)

Needles: One #10½ (6.5mm) circular needle, 24" (61cm) long, *or size needed to obtain gauge*

Gauge: 18 sts = 4" (10cm) in pattern stitch

Other supplies: Yarn needle, stitch marker, 4 yards 4-inch-wide satin blanket binding

NOTE: Blanket binding is packaged 4" (10cm) wide, folded over to make a 2" (5cm) strip.

---

cc = contrasting color ♦ **K** = knit ♦ **mc** = main color ♦ **st(s)** = stitch(es)
St st = stockinette stitch

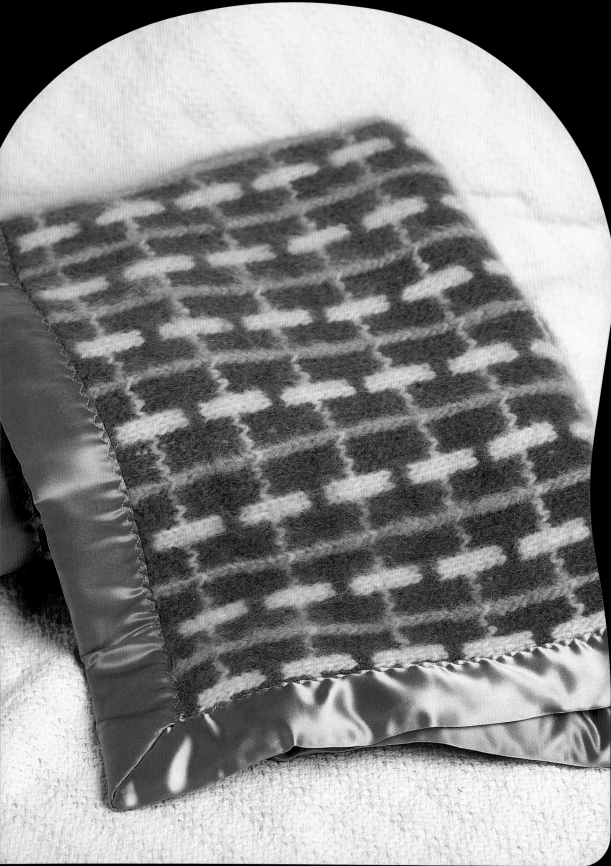

NOTE: The first and last 9 stitches of each round will form the selvedges and be hidden under the blanket binding when the project is finished. About 2 inches at the top and bottom of the blanket will also be bound.

With cc A, cast on 144 stitches. To mark the end of the round, place stitch marker on needle.

Round 1: K9, then, working in St st, follow the Plaid Chart on facing page, beginning at the bottom right. Repeat the 9 sts of the pattern 14 times, then K9 in cc A.

Next rounds: Continue to follow the chart, slipping the marker at the end of each round.

End with Round 18 of the pattern when the piece measures approximately 33" (84cm).

Turn the work inside out and weave any remaining loose ends into the wrong side of the work.

Locate the point where rows began and ended as you were knitting and run a loose basting stitch from top to bottom to mark a cutting line.

With a sewing machine, stitch lines ¼" (6mm) from both sides of the basting thread, using a zigzag stitch.

Carefully cut the fabric between the two lines of zigzag stitching, and lay the blanket out flat.

Place the blanket in your washing machine, and add other items to make a comfortably full load. (You can use normal household laundry, or fill out the load with bath towels.)

Allow the washer to fill with water, using the HOT setting.

Add laundry detergent as directed on the product label.

Run the washer through the complete wash-spin-rinse-spin cycle. Remove blanket and spread flat on a bath towel to dry, smoothing out any wrinkles and pulling it firmly to square up corners. (Do not machine dry.)

When blanket is completely dry, place it with right side up, and use a cat brush to fluff up the fibers and soften the surface. Brush lengthwise until you achieve the desired effect.

Pin the blanket binding in place by sandwiching the blanket inside the folded binding along the bottom, top, and side edges, using mitered folds to turn the corners. (See the illustration below.) Baste the binding in place about ¼" (6mm) from the edge of the binding.

Using a zigzag stitch, machine-stitch the binding to the blanket. Be sure to catch both sides of the binding with the stitches.

PLAID CHART

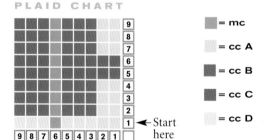

| = mc |
| = cc A |
| = cc B |
| = cc C |
| = cc D |

←Start here

Mitered corner

Tips for Handling Multiple Yarns

For most rounds, the selvedge will be knit using cc A yarn. However, in each repetition of the pattern, Rounds 5, 6, 14, and 15 begin and end with cc C instead of cc A. When you change from cc A to cc C and back again for Rounds 5, 7, 14, and 16, make the color change at the beginning of the round – that is, in the middle of the selvedge. Since the selvedge will be cut down the middle, you won't have to weave in the ends of the yarn. For other color changes, weave ends into the wrong side of the blanket.

Each round uses two or three colors of yarn. Carry all the colors used in a round through the whole round. Keeping carried yarn loose is particularly important when you are planning to felt a knitted project – you don't want the carried yarn to shrink more than the knitted fabric and cause the fabric to bunch up. For sections where the yarn must be carried more than three stitches, catch the carried yarn with the working yarn on the wrong side of the blanket every three stitches. For more information on working with multiple colors, see Colorful Effects, pages 19–21.

Patchwork Blankie

Designed by Gwen Steege, Williamstown, MA

This cheerful patchwork blanket is sure to become baby's favorite naptime carry-along. Lined with soft cotton flannel and trimmed with silky satin ribbon loops, it's not only colorful but also a tactile delight. We show it knitted in simple stockinette stitch in washable wool; it could also be made with a sport-weight cotton. If you would like a larger blanket, simply knit additional blocks and/or add more blocks across the row.

Finished measurements: 20" (51cm) square, including ribbon trim

Yarn: Dale of Norway Daletta, 100% machine-washable wool, fingering weight

60 yds (54m) mc (pale yellow #2014)

60 yds (54m) cc A (lilac #4814)

60 yds (54m) cc B (natural white #0020)

60 yds (54m) cc C (French blue #5813)

60 yds (54m) cc D (lichen #9725)

Needles

One set #4 (3.5mm) straight needles, *or size needed to obtain gauge*

Size E4 (#.5mm) bamboo or aluminum crochet hook

Gauge: 24 sts = 4" (10cm) on #4 (3.5mm) needles in St st

Other supplies: Yarn needle, 5 yarn bobbins (optional), 1 yd (1m) cotton flannel for lining, 7 yds (6m) of 1" (2.5cm) satin ribbon in a variety of colors, 1 skein of silk embroidery floss

---

K = knit ◆ **P** = purl ◆ **sl** = slip ◆ **st(s)** = stitch(es) ◆ **St st** = stockinette stitch

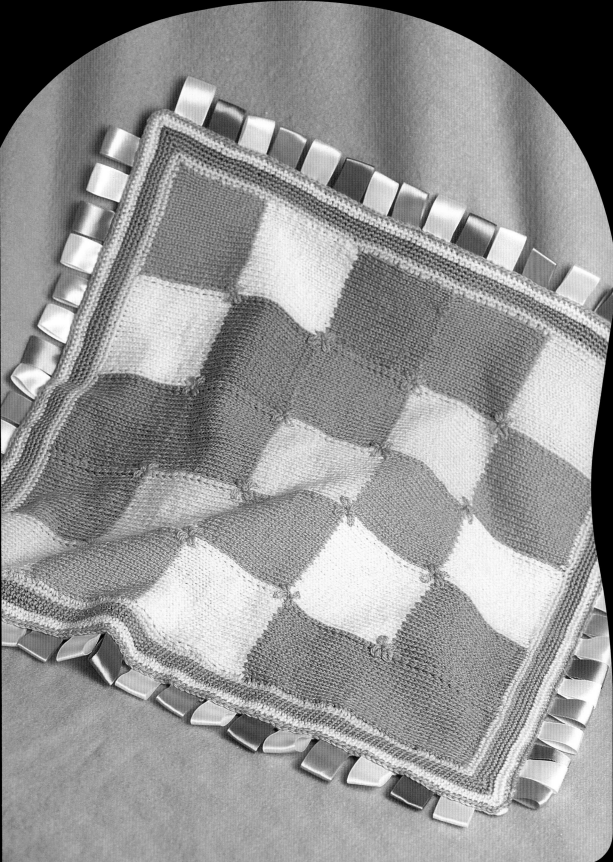

KNITTING THE FIRST COLOR BAND

NOTE: See Colorful Effects, pages 19–21. Before beginning each color band, fill 5 bobbins with 12 yds (11m) of yarn, each in a different color.

With mc, cast on 105 sts.

Row 1: K21 in mc, K21 in cc A, K21 in cc B, K21 in cc C, K21 in cc D. This sets up the blocks of color for the first color band.

Row 2: P21 in cc D, P21 in cc C, P21 in cc B, P21 in cc A, P21 in mc. Twist the yarn at the color changes to avoid gaps in the work, and leave the old color bobbins behind as you work across the row. Note that you must always make the yarn twists on the wrong side of the work.

Continue in St st in this color pattern until the block measures 3½" (9cm), ending with a wrong-side row.

KNITTING THE SECOND COLOR BAND

NOTE: In the second color band, each block of color moves one square to the left. To avoid having to cut the yarn and weave in the ends, carry each color — except for cc D, which was on the left border in the first band — along the back of the work to its new location.

Row 1: Cut cc D at the left-hand side of the work, leaving an end to weave back in. Join cc D at the beginning of the row and use it to K21. (Carry mc yarn behind the work, catching it with the working yarn every third st.)

K21 in mc, carrying cc A behind the work.

K21 in cc A, carrying cc B behind the work.

K21 in cc B, carrying cc C behind the work.

K21 in cc C.

Continue in St st in this color pattern until the block measures 3½" (9cm), ending with a wrong-side row. Remember to twist the yarn at all the color changes.

KNITTING THE THIRD COLOR BAND

Row 1: Cut cc C at the left-hand side of the work, leaving an end to weave back in. Join cc C at the beginning of the row and use it to K21. Carry cc D yarn behind the work, catching it with the working yarn every third st.

K21 in cc D, carrying mc behind the work.

K21 in mc, carrying cc A behind the work.

K21 in cc A, carrying cc B behind the work.

K21 in cc B.

Continue in St st in this color pattern until the block measures 3½" (9cm), ending with a wrong-side row.

Row 1: Cut cc B at the left-hand side of the work, leaving an end to weave back in. Join cc B at the beginning of the row and use it to K21. Carry cc C yarn behind the work, catching it with the working yarn every third st.

K21 in cc C, carrying cc D behind the work.

K21 in cc D, carrying mc behind the work.

K21 in mc, carrying cc A behind the work.

K21 in cc A.

Continue in St st in this color pattern until the block measures 3½" (9cm), ending with a wrong-side row.

Row 1: Cut cc A at the left-hand side of the work, leaving an end to weave back in. Join cc A at the beginning of the row and use it to K21. Carry cc B yarn behind the work, catching it with the working yarn every third st.

K21 in cc B, carrying cc C behind the work.

K21 in cc C, carrying cc D behind the work.

K21 in cc D, carrying mc behind the work.

K21 in mc.

Continue in St st in this color pattern until the block measures 3½" (9cm), ending with a wrong-side row. With mc, cast off.

Rows 1–2: With mc and a size E4 (3.5mm) crochet hook, work 2 rows of single crochet around the entire edge of the blanket, working 3 single crochets in the stitches at each corner.

Rows 3–4: Break working yarn, leaving enough tail to weave in, join cc D, and repeat Rows 1–2.

Rows 5–6: Break working yarn, leaving enough tail to weave in, join cc C, and repeat Rows 1–2.

Rows 7–8: Break working yarn, leaving enough tail to weave in, join cc B, and repeat Rows 1–2.

Row 9: Break working yarn, leaving enough tail to weave in, join cc A, and repeat Row 1. At the end of the row, draw the working end through the last loop to finish.

FINISHING

Weave in any loose ends on the wrong side of the blanket.

Block the work, following the directions on page 21.

Measure and cut a piece of cotton flannel for the lining, 2" longer and wider than knitted piece.

Turn a 1" (2.5cm) hem on all sides of the flannel. Press.

Cut the ribbon into 4" (10cm) lengths. Fold each length in half and pin it to the wrong side of the lining hem, allowing the folded edge to extend beyond the folded edge of the hem by about 1½" (4cm). (See illustration at right.) Distribute the colors randomly, as desired, placing two ribbons within each color block and positioning one over the join between colors.

Machine-stitch the ribbons in place, running the stitching about ⅛" (3mm) inside the folded edge of the hem.

With the wrong sides together, pin the blanket to the lining. Use strong sewing thread to slip stitch the edges of the blanket and lining together.

Place the blanket on a flat surface. Making sure that both knitted top and lining are smooth, pin the layers together at the center of each color block.

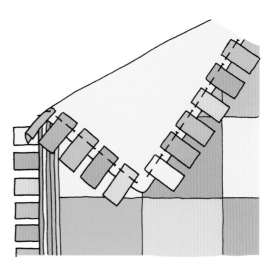

Attaching the ribbons

Lazy Daisies & French Knots

Use three strands of embroidery floss to make a four-petaled lazy daisy in each corner of each color block. When beginning the stitch, bring the needle from the back of the quilt, leaving a 3-inch (7.5cm) end. Complete the stitch by making a French knot in the middle of the daisy, then bring the needle back through the center to the wrong side, about ⅛" (3mm) away from the first end. Break off, leaving a 3-inch (7.5cm) end. Tie the ends in a square knot. Trim them to about ¾" (2cm).

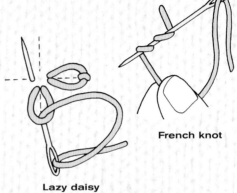

French knot

Lazy daisy

Primary Geometrics

Designed by Barbara Telford, Woodsmoke Woolworks

Many observers notice that bold color contrasts and geometric shapes like those in this pattern are especially appealing to babies and may even aid eye development. The blanket is made up of nine squares that are knitted separately in stockinette stitch, then joined by grafting or overcasting. A knitted border frames the central panel. This is a good take-along project, since you work on just one 9-inch square at a time.

Finished measurements: 32" (82cm) square

Yarn: Brown Sheep Lamb's Pride Superwash, 100% wool, worsted weight

430 yds (387m) mc (White Frost)
430 yds (387m) cc A (Navy Night)
430 yds (387m) cc B (Red Baron)
430 yds (387m) cc C (Sunflower)

Needles

Five #7 (4.5mm) circular needles, maximum length available, *or size needed to obtain gauge*

Set of five #7 (4.5mm) dp needles, *or same as above*

Gauge: 20 sts = 4" (10cm) on #7 (4.5mm) needles in St st

Other supplies: Yarn needle, stitch markers, crochet hook (size G/6), cotton waste yarn

---

cc = contrasting color ◆ **dp** = double pointed ◆ **inc** = increase ◆ **mc** = main color
rnd(s) = round(s) ◆ **st(s)** = stitch(es) ◆ **St st** = stockinette stitch

MAKING A SQUARE

Refer to Primary Geometrics Charts on pages 114 and 115 for color order. Begin each chart at the top (line 1). Work three of each of the three designs. Carry colors as you knit around, wrapping one yarn around the other for carries longer than 3 stitches (see Colorful Effects, pages 19–20).

With the dp needles and the color shown in the chart, cast on 4 sts.

Round 1: Inc 1 in each of 4 purl sts. You will have 8 sts.

Distribute the sts evenly among four needles and begin knitting in the round. You will start with 2 sts on each needle. For each round below, repeat instructions on each needle.

Round 2: Inc 1 in each of 2 knit sts. You will have 4 sts on each needle. The first st is the corner st. The increase at the beginning of the increase rows will be in the stitch following the corner stitch. NOTE: The increase stitch should always be the same color as the one following it.

Round 3: K1, inc 1, knit to last st, inc 1. You will have 6 sts on each needle.

Round 4: Knit even for the entire round.

Continue to follow the chart pattern and increase in the first and last sts on each needle in three rounds out of every four for the remainder of each square, until you have 48 sts on each needle.

The circle pattern has bobbles in Rounds 10 and 29. See Making Bobbles, page 114, for instructions.

After completing the final round shown on the chart, cast off purlwise if you plan to sew the squares together. See also Grafting, page 112, for another option.

ASSEMBLING THE CENTER PANEL

Join the squares together following the layout shown in the photo of the finished project, page 109. Either sew them, right sides together, or graft (see page 112). Make three strips of three squares each and then join the strips together in the same way.

MAKING THE BORDER

With four circular needles and cc A, pick up and knit every st on every side. You will have 144 sts on each needle. Knit in the round with the circular needles, just as you did with the dp needles for the individual squares.

Round 1: K1, inc 1, knit to last st, inc 1. You will have 146 sts on each needle.

Round 2: K1, inc 1, knit to last st, inc 1. You will have 148 sts on each needle.

Round 3: K1, inc 1, knit to last st, inc 1. You will have 150 sts on each needle.

Round 4: Knit even for the entire round.

Round 5: Switch to a Checkerboard Pattern (page 115) of 3 mc and 3 cc B and knit even for the entire round. You will have 150 sts on each needle.

Round 6: Continuing the Checkerboard Pattern, K1, inc 1, knit to last st, inc 1. You will have 152 sts on each needle.

Round 7: K1, inc 1, knit to last st, inc 1. You will have 154 sts on each needle.

Round 8: K1, inc 1, knit to last st, inc 1. You will have 156 sts on each needle.

Round 9: Switch back to cc A, and knit to end of round.

Round 10: P1, inc 1, purl to last st, inc 1. You will have 158 sts on each needle.

Round 11: K1, inc 1, knit to last st, inc 1. You will have 160 sts on each needle.

Round 12: P1, inc 1, purl to last st, inc 1. You will have 162 sts on each needle.

Cast off purlwise, cut the yarn, and weave in all the ends.

Grafting

Although you can join the squares of this blanket together with hand stitching, grafting (Kitchener's Stitch) is a neater, less conspicuous method. If you plan to graft the squares together, do not cast off at the end of each square, but slide the stitches onto a piece of waste yarn. When you are ready to join, put the stitches for two squares back onto needles, including the corner stitches at both ends of each square. Place the squares with wrong sides together. Follow the directions for Kitchener's Stitch on page 113.

Graft the squares together in strips and then graft the strips together in the same way. **Note:** You will probably have to work on one square at a time unless you have very long needles.

Kitchener Stitch

1. Hold two fabric layers together with purl sides facing. Using a needle, draw yarn through first stitch of front needle as if to knit; slip stitch off.

2. Draw yarn through second stitch of front needle as if to purl; leave stitch on needle.

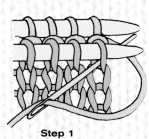

Step 1

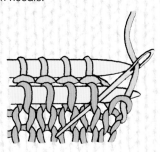

Step 2

3. Draw yarn through first stitch of back needle as if to purl; slip stitch off.

4. Draw yarn through second stitch of back needle as if to knit; leave stitch on. Repeat Steps 1–4 until no stitches remain on needles.

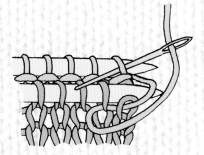

Step 3

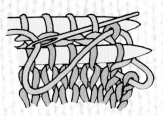

Step 4

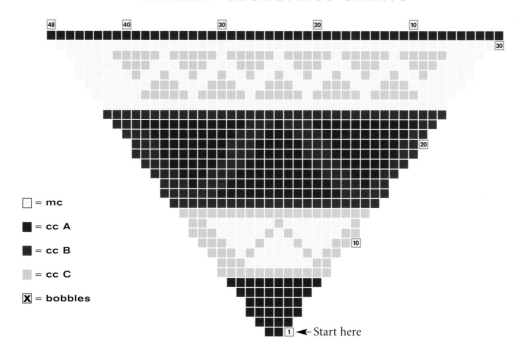

□ = mc

■ = cc A

■ = cc B

▦ = cc C

X = bobbles

Making Bobbles

The design at the right has bobbles knitted into the patterns (marked with an "X"). Bobbles are made by knitting several stitches into a single stitch, working on only these expanded stitches for one or more rows, and reducing them back into a single stitch.

To make a round bobble, with mc knit 4 sts into the marked st (knit into the front, back, front, and back again). Turn and P4, then turn again and K4tog through the back of the loop. (For the purl row, you may find that knitting the 4 sts backward, from the right needle to the left, gets you less tangled up than turning and purling them.) Using the row color, pick up and knit the st you originally knitted into, then pass the bobble st over it.

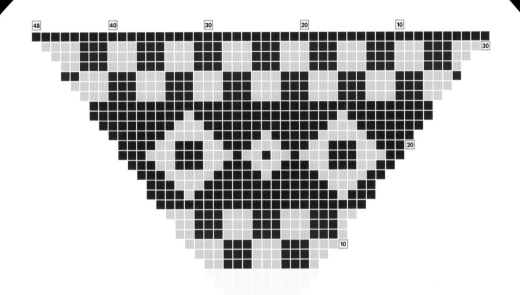

1 ◄ Start here

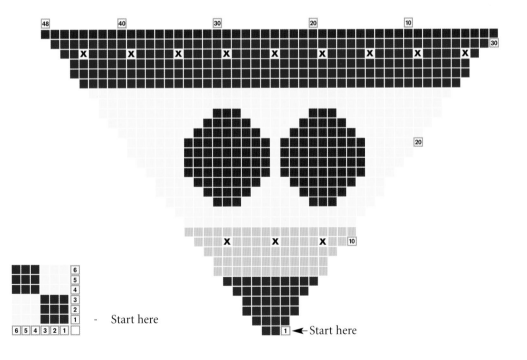

- Start here

1 ◄ Start here

Sweethearts

Designed by Beverly Galeskas, Fiber Trends

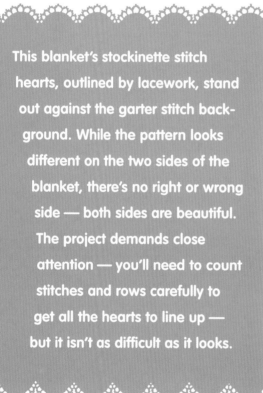

This blanket's stockinette stitch hearts, outlined by lacework, stand out against the garter stitch background. While the pattern looks different on the two sides of the blanket, there's no right or wrong side — both sides are beautiful. The project demands close attention — you'll need to count stitches and rows carefully to get all the hearts to line up — but it isn't as difficult as it looks.

Sizes and finished measurements:
Small: 30" by 36" (76cm by 91.5cm)
Medium: 38" by 44" (96.5cm by 112cm)
Yarn: Cotton Clouds Softball, 100% cotton, double-knit weight
Small: 1050 yds (945m) (Heliotrope)
Medium: 1650 yds (1485m)
Needles: One #7 (4.5mm) circular needle, 29" (74cm) long, *or size needed to obtain gauge*
Gauge: 18 sts = 4" (10cm) on #7 (4.5mm) needle in St st
Other supplies: Yarn needle, row counter.

---

ddecL = left double decrease ◆ **ddecR** = right double decrease ◆ **K** = knit ◆ **K2tog** = knit 2 stitches together ◆ **P** = purl ◆ **psso** = pass slip stitch over ◆ **sl** = slip ◆ **ssk** = slip, slip, knit 2 together ◆ **st(s)** = stitch(es) ◆ **St st** = stockinette stitch ◆ **YO** = yarn over

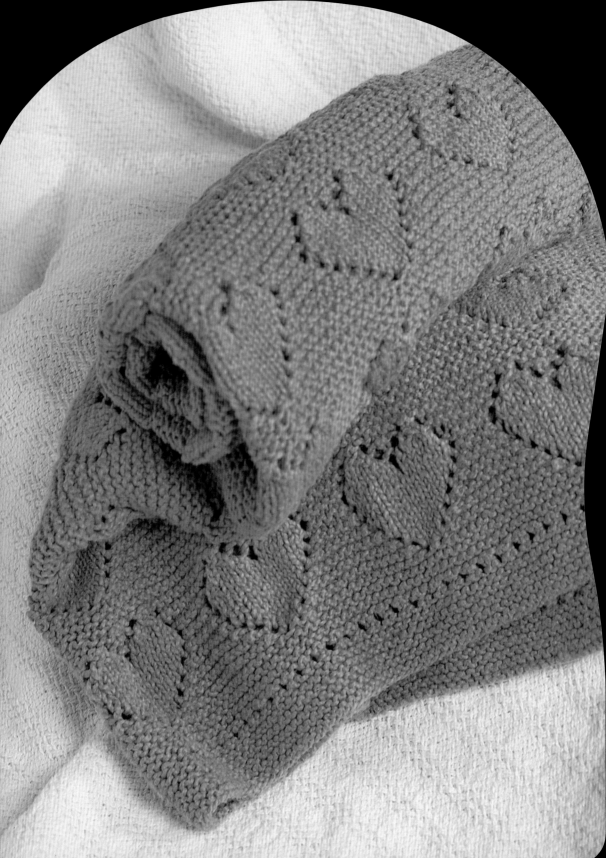

KNITTING THE BOTTOM BORDER	SMALL	MEDIUM
With #7 (4.5mm) circular needle, cast on	135 sts	169 sts
Rows 1–11: Knit each row to last st, sl 1.		
Row 12: K6, *YO, K2tog; repeat from * to last 5 sts; K4, sl 1. You will still have the same number of sts you started with.	135 sts	169 sts
KNITTING THE HEART PATTERN		
NOTE: You may find it helpful to refer to the Sweethearts Chart on page 121. The chart provides visual symbols for the instructions in this section. Rows 13–15 (chart lines 1–3): Knit each row to last st, sl 1.		
Row 16: K6, YO, ssk, knit to last 8 sts, K2tog, YO, K5, sl 1.		
Rows 17–19: Knit each row to last st, sl 1.		
Row 20: K6, YO, ssk, K6, *K2tog, YO, K1, YO, ssk, K12; repeat from * to last 19 sts; K2tog, YO, K1, YO, ssk, K6, K2tog, YO, K5, sl 1.		
Row 21: K15, *P3, K14; repeat from * to last 18 sts; P3, K14, sl 1.		
Row 22: K13, *K2tog, YO, K3, YO, ssk, K10; repeat from * to last 20 sts; K2tog, YO, K3, YO, ssk, K12, sl 1.		
Row 23: K14, *P5, K12; repeat from * to last 19 sts; P5, K13, sl 1.		
Row 24: K6, YO, ssk, K4, *K2tog, YO, K5, YO, ssk, K8; repeat from * to last 21 sts; K2tog, YO, K5, YO, ssk, K4, K2tog, YO, K5, sl 1.		
Row 25: K13, *P7, K10; repeat from * to last 20 sts; P7, K12, sl 1.		
Row 26: K11, *K2tog, YO, K7, YO, ssk, K6; repeat to last 22 sts; K2tog, YO, K7, YO, ssk, K10, sl 1.		
Row 27: K12, *P9, K8; repeat from * to last 21 sts; P9, K11, sl 1.		

Double Decreases

When you're making lacy patterns, you need to work the decreases carefully so the eyelet holes will appear exactly where you want them. Double decreases – making holes to the left and right of a stitch – are the trickiest of all. Here are the techniques for making double decreases with the stitch in between slanting to the left or right.

Left double decrease (ddecL): Sl 1, K2tog, psso.

Right double decrease (ddecR): Ssk, slip this stitch to left needle, pass the next stitch over it and off the needle, return stitch to right needle.

	SMALL	MEDIUM
Row 28: K6, YO, ssk, K2, *K2tog, YO, K9, YO, ssk, K4; repeat to last 23 sts; K2tog, YO, K9, YO, ssk, K2, K2tog, YO, K5, sl 1.		
Row 29: K11, *P11, K6; repeat from * to last 22 sts; P11, K10, sl 1.		
Row 30: K9, *K2tog, YO, K11, YO, ssk, K2; repeat from * to last 24 sts; K2tog, YO, K11, YO, ssk, K8, sl 1.		
Row 31: K10, *P13, K4; repeat from * to last 23 sts; P13, K9, sl 1.		
Row 32: K6, YO, ssk, K2, *YO, K2tog, K4, YO, K2tog, K3, ssk, YO, K4; repeat from * to last 23 sts; YO, K2tog, K4, YO, K2tog, K3, ssk, YO, K2, K2tog, YO, K5, sl 1.		
Row 33: K11, *P5, K1, P5, K6; repeat from * to last 22 sts; P5, K1, P5, K10, sl 1.		
Row 34: K11, *YO, K2tog, K1, ssk, YO, K1, YO, K2tog, K1, ssk, YO, K6; repeat from * to last 22 sts; YO, K2tog, K1, ssk, YO, K1, YO, K2tog, K1, ssk, YO, K10, sl 1.		
Row 35: K12, *P3, K3, P3, K8; repeat from * to last 21 sts; P3, K3, P3, K11, sl 1.		

	SMALL	MEDIUM
Row 36: K6, YO, ssk, K4, *YO, ddecL, YO, K3, YO, ddecR, YO, K8; repeat from * to last 21 sts; YO, ddecL, YO, K3, YO, ddecR, YO, K4, K2tog, YO, K5, sl 1. (See page 119 for instructions on ddecL and ddecR.)		
Repeat Rows 13–36	11 more times	13 more times
Repeat Rows 13–19 once more		
KNITTING THE TOP BORDER		
Row 1: K6, *YO, K2tog; repeat from * to last 5 sts; K4, sl 1.		
Rows 2–10: Knit each row to last st, sl 1.		
Cast off loosely, knitwise.		
FINISHING UP		
Cut yarn and work the ends in carefully so the blanket will be reversible.		

Garter Stitch Edging

Garter stitch produces an unfinished-looking edge. On a blanket or other piece where the edge will be visible, use this technique to make a cleaner edge.

Slip the last stitch of each row with the yarn behind the work. When you turn the work over to start the next row, insert the needle into the first stitch, take the yarn across the front of this stitch to the back, then knit the stitch.

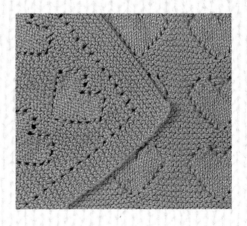

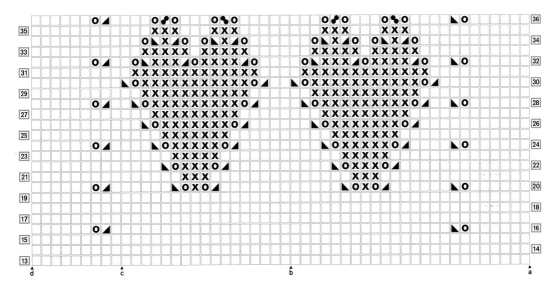

☐ = Knit on right side and knit on wrong side

X = Knit on right side and purl on wrong side

◢ = K2tog

◣ = ssk (slip, slip, knit)

O = YO (yarn over)

◥ = left slanting double decrease (slip 1, K2tog, psso)

◤ = right slanting double decrease (ssk, put this stitch back onto left needle and pass the next stitch over it and off the needle; return stitch to right needle)

Line-by-line instructions for the Sweethearts blanket are provided on pages 118–120. You may also use the above chart for guidance:

NOTE: With yarn in the back, slip the last stitch of each row.

1. Work Rows 1–12 following instructions on page 118, then begin chart on Row 13 (a wrong-side row).

2. Work wrong-side (odd-numbered) rows following the chart from left to right. Begin by working stitches between points d and c, then repeat the stitches

between points c and b until you come to the last 24 stitches. End with the stitches between points b and a.

3. Work right-side (even-numbered) rows following the chart from right to left. Begin by working the stitches between points a and b, then repeat the stitches between points b and c until you get to the last 9 stitches. End with the stitches between points c and d.

4. Repeat Rows 13–36 twelve times for small size and fourteen times for medium size, then Rows 13–19 once more. End by following instructions on page 120 for top border.

Contributing Designers

In her 20 years of enthusiastic knitting, **Dori Betjemann** has yet to follow a pattern as written. Modifying, tweaking, trial and error, and study gradually led to comfort with the math of knitting instructions. At some point, she realized she no longer needed patterns and was free to indulge fully in the fun of knitting and publishing her own ideas. For five years she has been the knitting instructor at the Hill Institute in Florence, Massachusetts, where she conducts weekly classes for more than 50 beginner through advanced adult students. She also provides private lessons for individuals. Working part time at WEBS, a large, fast-paced yarn store in Northampton, Massachusetts, keeps her in touch with what's new in the industry and gives her a lot of practice in solving knitting problems. e-mail: betj@attbi.com

Kathleen Case learned to knit as a child, but she did not become seriously interested in the craft until she began knitting socks and scarves in high school, where students were allowed to knit during classes! She has been making variations of the basketweave blanket since she knit one for her first child many years ago, always varying the size, yarn, and pattern to keep it interesting.

Northampton Wools
11 Pleasant Street
Northampton, MA 01060
(413) 586-4331
e-mail: NohoKnit@aol.com

Since 1988, **Linda Daniels** has owned and operated Northampton Wools, a full-service retail store offering knitting classes and a wide selection of yarns from around the world. *Interweave Knits* has featured many of her patterns, and she designed and knit actor Michael Caine's vest and several sweaters for the hit movie *The Cider House Rules.*

Ruth Fresia has been knitting since she was seven. She has taught knitting workshops; designed knitting patterns for Ulltex, a yarn wholesaler and mail-order company; and won prizes for design at CraftAdventure, a regional craft show. e-mail: rj.fresia@verizon.net

Fiber Trends
P.O. Box 7266
East Wenatchee, WA 98802
(509) 884-8631
www.fibertrends.com

Beverly Galeskas is the owner and founder of Fiber Trends Pattern Company. Along with other designing, Bev is always looking for new ways to use the fascinating technique of knitting and felting (fulling) to create unique garments, accessories, and toys. She has taught classes at TNNA, Stitches, and many other knitting and fiber shows. Fiber Trends patterns are available at yarn stores across North America. An extensive listing of stores can be found on her Web site; in an effort to support those stores, she does not offer direct mail order. "I believe my experiences of learning to knit as an adult and then teaching beginning knitting in my yarn store were the best training for writing patterns for others," she says.

Sakonnet Purls/Designs by Louise
3988 Main Road
Tiverton, RI 02878
(888) 624-9902
www.sakonnetpurls.com

Louise Silverman comes from a family of knitting and needlework designers. As the owner of Sakonnet Purls, one of the largest knitting stores in the United States, she found the need to create patterns that take the mystery out of knitting. She calls her designs "Friendly Patterns for the Average Knitter." More than 40 Designs by Louise patterns are available in knitting and needlework stores nationwide. Louise's daughters work at Sakonnet Purls, continuing the family tradition.

Gwen Steege, an avid knitter for more than 50 years, also enjoys spinning, dyeing, and weaving wool from her Romney sheep. She is an editor at Storey Publishing and lives in Williamstown, Massachusetts.

Woodsmoke Woolworks
1335 Route 102
Upper Gagetown, NB E5M 1R5
Canada
(506) 488-2044
e-mail: woodsmke@nbnet.nb.ca

Barbara Telford doesn't remember not knowing how to knit. A member of the Canadian Knitwear Designers Association and a juried member of the New Brunswick Craft Council, she runs Woodsmoke Woolworks, a farm-based knitwear and design shop. She won the New Brunswick Craft Council's Oudemans Christmas Choice Award in 2002 for the ingenuity of her knitted hat collection. Her unique work is outstanding for its originality and her ability to manipulate wool to produce witty and lively designs. "I don't know where the designs came from," she says, "but I'm glad they came."

Acknowledgments

Many thanks to

The knitters and test knitters who helped make the projects for this book:
Dori Betjemann, Rebecca Bienn, Ann Burch, Linda Burt, Kathleen Case,
Mary Ellen Czerniak, Linda Daniels, Diana Foster, Ruth Fresia, Beverly Galeskas,
Mary Johnson, Danielle Kadinoff, Alison Kolesar, Margaret Radcliffe, Rita Riley,
Louise Silverman, Barbara Telford, and Sarah Thurston.

The companies that supplied yarn:
Brown Sheep Company of Mitchell, Nebraska
Cotton Clouds of Safford, Arizona
Dale of Norway of Waukesha, Wisconsin
Plymouth Yarn Company of Bristol, Pennsylvania
Tahki Stacy Charles of Brooklyn, New York

The yarn stores that offered invaluable advice:
The Naked Sheep, Bennington, Vermont
Northampton Wools, Northampton, Massachusetts
WEBS, Northampton, Massachusetts
Woolcott & Co., Cambridge, Massachusetts

Index

Page numbers in **bold** indicate a table or box.
Page numbers *italics* indicate a photo or illustration.

Other Storey Titles You Will Enjoy

Knit Baby Head & Toes! edited by Gwen Steege
Hardcover
ISBN 1-58017-494-9
Full-color photographs and
illustrations throughout
128 pages

Knit Hats! edited by Gwen Steege
Hardcover
ISBN 1-58017-482-5
Full-color photographs and
illustrations throughout
96 pages

Knit Mittens! by Robin Hansen
Hardcover
ISBN 1-58017-483-3
Full-color photographs and
illustrations throughout
128 pages

Knit Christmas Stockings! edited by Gwen Steege
Hardcover
ISBN 1-58017-505-8
Full-color photographs and
illustrations throughout
136 pages

Available wherever books are sold.